A PARENT'S GUIDE TO

ATTENTION DEFICIT DISORDERS

THE CHILDREN'S HOSPITAL OF PHILADELPHIA

A PARENT'S GUIDE TO

ATTENTION DEFICIT DISORDERS

Foreword by
C. EVERETT KOOP, M.D.

LISA J. BAIN

A Delta Book
Published by
Dell Publishing
a division of
Bantam Doubleday Dell Publishing Group, Inc.
666 Fifth Avenue
New York, New York 10103

Grateful acknowledgment is made for permission to reprint the following:

Material from *American Psychiatric Association: Diagnostic and Statistical Manual of Mental Disorders, Third Edition, Revised.* American Psychiatric Association, Washington, D.C., 1987.

Conners Teacher Rating Scale. Multi-Health Systems, 908 Niagara Falls Blvd., North Tonawanda, New York 14120-2060.

Library of Congress Cataloging-in-Publication Data

Bain, Lisa J.
   A parent's guide to attention deficit disorders / Lisa J. Bain : foreword by
C. Everett Koop.
      p.   cm.
   "A Delta book"—T.p. verso.
   At head of title: The Children's Hospital of Philadelphia.
   Includes bibliographical references.
   ISBN 0-385-30031-X (pbk.) : $10.00
   1. Attention deficit disorders—Popular works.   I. Children's Hospital of
Philadelphia.   II. Title.   III. Title: Attention deficit disorders.
   [DNLM: 1. Attention Deficit Disorder with Hyperactivity.   WS 340
B162p]
RJ496.A86B35   1991
618.92'8589—dc20   91-24652
                                                                          CIP

Manufactured in the United States of America
Published simultaneously in Canada

September 1991

10 9 8 7 6 5 4

RRH

Contents

Foreword

Having spent my entire medical career at The Children's Hospital of Philadelphia, it is relevant to me both personally and professionally to introduce the first in a series of books produced under the aegis of the Hospital for the improvement of children's lives.

Intended as a resource for parents, this book concerns itself with children whose behavior and learning difficulties relate to their ability to pay attention, sit still, and focus on important tasks. In today's parlance, they are identified as having attention deficit–hyperactivity disorder, or ADHD. The book draws from the expertise and experience of a group of pediatricians, psychiatrists, psychologists, neurologists, and social workers who work with children identified as having ADHD at The Children's Hospital of Philadelphia, the Philadelphia Child Guidance Clinic, and the Children's Seashore House.

The book's goal is to help answer questions and clarify issues about ADHD and help parents to understand their children—an especially daunting task for families in which both parents work, or in which there is a single parent.

Despite the fact that ADHD has been, and continues to be, a widely researched subject, there is no universal agreement among those in the field about what constitutes ADHD, what causes it, or how it should best be treated. In fact, there remains some controversy about whether the disorder truly exists, although most experts agree that many children do have difficulty functioning and can benefit from some intervention. Proper identification of such children is needed in order to provide appropriate services.

One of the factors that contributes to the lack of clarity about the disorder is its variability. Each ADHD child experiences a unique constellation of personality and temperamental traits and ADHD-related symptoms. Many have learning as well as behavioral difficulties. As a result, each child must be considered individually in order that appropriate management strategies can be developed. These interventions may include a combination of medication, behavior therapy, family therapy, and educational intervention. This book suggests a multimodal approach, which appears to offer children significant benefits over the long term.

Managing ADHD involves more than treating the child, however. The child's entire family often experiences increased stress, anger, and guilt that can eat away at the marriage and the ability of the family to function harmoniously. Thus, treatment should be directed at all members of the family in order that their social and emotional health is maintained. Parents must learn to take care of themselves at the same time that they are trying to care for their children. In addition, parents of children with ADHD need to learn all they can about the disorder so that they can be effective advocates for their children. This book enables parents to acquire clearer understanding of the child with ADHD and to be sufficiently knowledgeable to find the best possible care.

C. Everett Koop, M.D.
Surgeon-in-Chief Emeritus
The Children's Hospital of Philadelphia

Preface

Every Tuesday at twelve thirty at a hospital in Philadelphia, a group of physicians, psychologists, psychiatrists, and social workers gather around a table to discuss the cases of children with attention deficit disorders. These health professionals come from three different institutions: The Children's Hospital of Philadelphia, the Philadelphia Child Guidance Clinic, and the Children's Seashore House. They join forces in order to provide a comprehensive evaluation and treatment program for children with the most common behavior problem seen in school-age children today.

At the meetings, these professionals share their different viewpoints and areas of expertise, and together they develop a management approach that meets the needs of each individual child. They consider the results of medical, psychological, and school evaluations that have been conducted and determine whether other evaluations are needed. They bring with them years of experience in working with children who have attention deficits or other behavioral problems.

As the writer of this book, I had the good fortune of being able to sit in on many of these meetings so that I might gain an appreciation for the many facets of this disorder. In addition, I met individually for many hours with these professionals and have relied heavily on their expertise. They worked with me to develop a book that would be both resourceful and supportive to parents.

The input of these professionals was complemented and reinforced by the cooperation and thoughtful input of many parents and children, some who let me sit in on their medical and psychological consultations. Their perspective provided the framework from which I have constructed this book. Their names have all been changed, but their stories are true.

Throughout this book, the terms *attention deficit disorder (ADD)* and *attention deficit–hyperactivity disorder (ADHD)* are used almost interchangeably. As explained in chapter 1, *ADHD* is the technical term that is currently used to describe the disorder. *ADD* is an older, more general and all-encompassing term that is commonly used by professionals and parents alike. It could apply to a child regardless of whether he or she has been identified under the current guidelines for ADHD or previous versions.

Acknowledgments

Marc S. Atkins, Ph.D.
Pediatric Psychologist, Children's Seashore House,
   The Children's Hospital of Philadelphia
Assistant Professor of Psychology in Pediatrics and
   Psychiatry, University of Pennsylvania School of
   Medicine

Mark L. Batshaw, M.D.
Physician-in-Chief, Children's Seashore House
Chief, Division of Child Development and Rehabilitation,
   The Children's Hospital of Philadelphia
W. T. Grant Professor of Pediatrics and Neurology,
   University of Pennsylvania School of Medicine

Peter H. Berman, M.D.
Director, Division of Neurology,
   The Children's Hospital of Philadelphia
Professor of Neurology and Pediatrics, University of
   Pennsylvania School of Medicine

Susan E. Levy, M.D.
Co-Director, Attention Deficit Hyperactivity Disorder
   Clinic and Clinical Attending Physician,
   Children's Seashore House
Associate Physician, The Children's Hospital of Philadelphia
Assistant Professor of Pediatrics, University of Pennsylvania
   School of Medicine

Marianne Mercugliano, M.D.
Attending Developmental Pediatrician, Attention Deficit
   Hyperactivity Disorder Clinic, Children's Seashore House,
   The Children's Hospital of Philadelphia
Assistant Professor of Pediatrics, University of Pennsylvania
   School of Medicine

Thomas J. Power, Ph.D. Pediatric Psychologist
Associate Director, Attention Deficit Hyperactivity
  Disorder Clinic, Children's Seashore House,
  The Children's Hospital of Philadelphia

Anthony L. Rostain, M.D.
Medical Director, Consultation Liaison Psychiatry Services,
  Philadelphia Child Guidance Clinic and
  The Children's Hospital of Philadelphia
Co-Director, Attention Deficit Hyperactivity Disorder
  Clinic, Children's Seashore House
Assistant Professor of Psychiatry and Pediatrics, University
  of Pennsylvania School of Medicine

Abbie Segal-Andrews, M.A.
Certified School Psychologist
Psychology Extern, Children's Seashore House

Alberto C. Serrano, M.D.
Medical Director, Philadelphia Child Guidance Clinic
Psychiatrist-in-Chief and Director, Psychiatry Division,
  The Children's Hospital of Philadelphia
Professor of Psychiatry and Pediatrics and Director,
  Division of Child and Adolescent Psychiatry, Department
  of Psychiatry, University of Pennsylvania School of
  Medicine

Jo Ann Sonis, ACSW, LSW
Clinical Social Worker, Attention Deficit Hyperactivity
  Disorder Clinic, Children's Seashore House

I would also like to thank several other people who made
this work possible. Shirley Bonnem, Vice President of Public
and Government Relations at The Children's Hospital of
Philadelphia, originated the idea for this book and, with the
help of her assistant Dorothy Barnes, guided it to completion. My editor at Dell, Emily Reichert, and literary agent,
Nancy Love, provided continual support and encouragement. And finally, thanks to my parents, for August.

Introduction

This book is about children who can't sit still, can't pay attention, and can't seem to fit into school or other structured activities. In years past, they might have been labeled hyperactive or hyperkinetic, or even brain damaged. Today they are diagnosed as having attention deficit–hyperactivity disorder (ADHD).

Attention deficits and hyperactivity can create many problems for children. In school, these children may have trouble listening, paying attention, and sitting still. They may have trouble learning—a problem that can be compounded by a specific learning disability that is not part of their attention deficit disorder or their hyperactivity. They less frequently enjoy the thrill of acquiring new knowledge. Their lack of success in this respect means that they miss out on receiving positive feedback from teachers and parents—the pats on the back and recognition of jobs well done that motivate other children to keep on trying. They may feel frustrated and angry and "bad." Other children may shun them.

ADHD takes its toll not only on the children themselves but on their families. Parents often feel that somehow they have failed in their duties. Mother and father may argue about how best to discipline the child. Siblings may resent the increased attention that the ADHD child receives. All in all, the family of an ADHD child bears an especially heavy load of stress that can eat away at the family structure and the marriage.

This book addresses many aspects of ADHD, not only its impact on children and families but the current medical and psychological thinking about its causes and treatment. It draws on the expertise of a multidisciplinary group of pediatricians, neurologists, child psychiatrists, psychologists, and social workers at The Children's Hospital of Philadelphia, the Philadelphia Child Guidance Clinic, and Children's Seashore House. It also draws from the experiences of many parents and children whose lives have been affected by ADHD. Although each family's story is different, they share many characteristics as well. Most parents feel frustrated by the lack of clear answers to their many questions about ADHD. Many feel guilty about medicating their children, even though it seems to help, and nearly all parents feel exhausted from constantly fighting to get what is best for their child, especially when they feel ill-equipped to mount that fight, as they often do. While no book can answer all the questions about ADHD, the goal of this book is to help clarify some of the issues and to help parents better understand and raise their children with ADHD.

THE CONTROVERSY OVER ADHD

Probably no other childhood behavior problem has been more extensively researched, yet as hotly debated, as ADHD. On one side, some experts see ADHD as a common psychiatric disorder that affects as many as 20 percent of all

school-age children. Others say that this is a myth, perpe-
trated primarily as a means of controlling undesirable behavior. Both these views can do a disservice to children who
have attentional and related behavioral problems. Some children's behavioral difficulties are not medical in origin but
arise from external causes, such as family squabbles or reactions to specific stressful situations. Treating these children as
if they suffered from a medical condition can divert attention
from the real sources of trouble. But for other children, inborn temperament does play a significant role in determining
behavior, and they truly do suffer from an inability to stay
seated or pay attention. Denying this can prevent the child
from obtaining treatment that can allow him* to live a happy,
productive life. Furthermore, it can undermine his sense of
self-worth and lead his parents to the mistaken conclusion
that their poor parenting has caused the behavioral difficulties.

The controversy surrounding ADHD arises from many
sources. Though the disorder has been widely researched, no
one yet knows why it occurs or what causes it. Specialists
differ as to the best way to treat it, and the medical, scientific,
and psychological communities often disagree even on what
characteristics should constitute a diagnosis of ADHD. But
while ADHD remains mysterious in many ways, the decades
of research overwhelmingly support the notion that there is
an inborn, physiological component to the disorder. Children
with ADHD are no longer thought to be "minimally brain
damaged," as they largely were in the 1940s, 1950s, and
1960s. Today, neuroscientists in the field focus on biochemical interactions within specific areas of the brain and hypothe-
size that an imbalance in certain neurochemicals may impair
normal levels of activity and attention.

* Throughout this book, the male pronoun is usually used to refer to
children with ADHD. It should be understood that many children with
ADHD are girls. But the overwhelming majority are boys, as we shall
see in chapters 1 and 3.

Biology may explain one piece of the ADHD puzzle, but no medical model can fully explain it. Modern medicine has led people to expect certainty—clear-cut causes, tests that can either confirm or deny diagnoses, and drugs that can cure or prevent a problem. But with ADHD, environmental and societal factors are also at work. A child's school situation—the academic demands placed on him, his teachers, friends, and classroom, and the playground structure—as well as his family interactions play a part in determining to what extent his attentional difficulties create problems. Moreover, the scientific description of the problem has changed over the years. In the 1980s, for example, the scientific community did a flip-flop on the issue of whether hyperactivity is an essential component of the disorder. This inability to pin down the description, some argue, indicates that there is no clearly definable syndrome at all, that these changing descriptions are simply repeated, failed efforts to categorize a disorder where no disorder exists. Some critics of ADHD's existence have even gone so far as to suggest that a conspiracy exists among the medical community, drug companies that manufacture the stimulants commonly used to treat these children, and teachers who don't want to or can't deal with rambunctious kids. Still others criticize current medical treatments of ADHD; the most vocal argue that overprescription of stimulant medication is leading to schools filled with zombielike children. According to these critics, the most commonly used drug, Ritalin (methylphenidate), has caused psychosis and depression and has even led to suicide. No wonder parents are frightened and some pediatricians are reluctant to treat!

Although the stories that these critics cite are few in number and often distorted, they nonetheless underscore the need for parents to be educated about and involved in the treatment of their children. Any drug can be overprescribed and misused if it is not given and monitored carefully. Parents need to know what to expect, what kinds of reactions to watch for, and how to get responses to their concerns.

THE DIFFERENT FACES OF ADHD

Much of the controversy and confusion about ADHD can be attributed to the disorder's heterogeneity. Consider the cases of two children who have been diagnosed with ADHD. The first, Danny, was a tornado practically from birth—always on the go, demanding attention, and getting into things. His mother recalls that at age four, Danny climbed to the top of her breakfront to retrieve some Halloween goodies, toppling the furniture and breaking her china collection. But Danny's parents never viewed him as "bad." He was delightful, a charmer, always laughing. At age four, Danny's parents took him to a psychologist for evaluation, expecting the expert to say that Danny's superior intelligence led him to be bored and restless. Instead, after a thorough evaluation, the doctor said that Danny had an attention deficit disorder and was hyperactive.

The second child, Alex, came to the ADHD clinic in fourth grade. He was falling behind in his schoolwork and seemed very discouraged and unhappy. His teachers reported few behavior problems in class, although they were frustrated by his lower-than-expected performance and seeming lack of motivation. They reported that he often seemed unable to concentrate and would miss many instructions they gave for assignments. When the psychologist met with him, Alex's eyes filled with tears as he spoke of his difficulties at school. His teachers didn't like him, he said, and he had trouble paying attention when homework was assigned. Like Danny, Alex was diagnosed as having ADHD.

Although Danny and Alex display distinctly different behaviors, they are by no means extreme examples. Yet their stories illustrate the range of behaviors that can result in a diagnosis of ADHD. Moreover, they serve to point out that the diagnosis captures only certain characteristics of a child's identity. It doesn't say whether he's good-natured, friendly, good or poor socially, bright, or sad. All it says is that he has a cluster of symptoms that involve his ability to pay attention, sit still, and focus on a task. In chapter 1, we discuss more fully the characteristics that distinguish a child with ADHD.

THE PROBLEM OF LABELING

Given the broad range of behaviors that are classified as ADHD-related, many parents may reasonably wonder about the importance and validity of having a diagnosis. Why subject a child to the diagnostic process when the results will almost certainly be imprecise? Moreover, having a child labeled with a psychiatric diagnosis may create a new set of difficulties. What assumptions will other people make—friends, teachers, family members—when they learn that the child "has ADHD"? Without getting to know him individually, will people assume he has problems and treat him as a problem child? Will he end up an outcast?

The ADHD label certainly can stigmatize a child, but it can also serve useful functions for everyone involved. The label can benefit parents in a number of ways. For parents who worry about what they might be doing wrong that has led to the child's difficulties, the label can relieve their guilt. Often, by the time a child's ADHD comes to the attention of professionals, the parents have endured years of built-up frustration, anger, and guilt. Labeling their child as having ADHD can help such parents view the problem from a different perspective; not "What did I do wrong?" but "What can I do to help?" For parents who have suspected all along that their child is more than simply "misbehaved" or "difficult," the label that confirms their suspicions can bolster their self-confidence.

The label can also help the child. His parents and teachers may let go of some of their anger at him when they come to understand that he is not being malicious or "bad," but that he lacks the tools he needs to conform to their expectations. Older children with ADHD may be relieved to find out that there is a reason that they feel so out of control at times, so unable to meet the expectations of their parents and teachers.

Receiving a label of ADHD also opens doors to myriad management strategies. Parents and children alike can turn their thoughts from resignation about their situation to hope about the future. Part II discusses the various approaches that can benefit children who have been diagnosed with ADHD.

Moreover, the ADHD label has a useful practical side. It tells schools and other institutions that this child has special needs that must be considered. It gives the educational, medical, and research communities a framework from which they can work toward a better understanding of the disorder and a refinement of the treatments. Finally, it gives insurance companies a diagnosis for which they will reimburse.

PARENT ADVOCACY

But in order to realize the positive side of labeling, parents need to take action. The label alone says very little about a child's individual persona, and it also says very little about the best way to manage his difficulties. Parents need to work with all the resources at their disposal to uncover the distinguishing characteristics of their child's disorder and to match his problems with appropriate actions.

You, as parents, are in the best position of anybody to know all the aspects of your child's problem, but in order to take action, you must first become educated about ADHD. You will be dealing with many people who know little about ADHD, and your expertise will be essential. Learn to speak the language of the professionals with whom you will come in contact.

This book is divided into three sections. Part I explains the current thinking about what ADHD is and isn't and how this thinking has evolved over the last ninety years; it provides the latest information about what might cause ADHD. Part II guides you through the various diagnostic and treatment options that you will encounter. Part III offers insight into what you can expect in the future and how you can best take care of your family's social and emotional needs, including your own.

This book reflects the goals of the professionals at The Children's Hospital of Philadelphia, the Philadelphia Child Guidance Clinic, and the Children's Seashore House (PCGC and CSH)—that you will gain a clearer perspective about your child and that this perspective and your knowledge of options will provide you with the tools you need to seek out the best care.

PART I
Educating Yourself

CHAPTER 1

The Child with ADHD

Defining ADHD has been and continues to be a vexing problem for behavioral scientists. Over the years, the definition has changed, the diagnostic criteria have been revised, and the questions have multiplied. But despite the seeming chaos in the field, a more refined and holistic picture is beginning to emerge. While pediatricians, psychologists, child psychiatrists, social workers, educators, and parents are far from agreeing on a unified theory, they are starting to see their views as compatible rather than opposing and to work together to find better solutions for children.

The name *attention deficit–hyperactivity disorder* sounds clear and definite, but scientists who study ADHD have been unable to pin down the abnormality's precise nature. They have ruled some things out: for example, no clear neurological impairment has been demonstrated for most children with ADHD, and no obvious disease exists. Nevertheless, most experts in the field do believe that there is something different and somewhat abnormal about the way the brain functions in a child with ADHD. They also know that the symptoms are not simply the result of ineffective parenting, although parenting does affect the nature and severity of the problems.

Currently, what can be said with some certainty is that

ADHD involves a set of behavioral characteristics that impair a child's ability to function in his or her environment. Though biologically based, these characteristics are influenced by psychological and social factors. None of these behavioral characteristics taken alone would necessarily be considered abnormal. But taken in combination, or because of their intensity or pervasiveness, or because of the nature of the child's environment, they can create problems in the classroom, home, and other places. Moreover, they initiate a spiral of problems. A child who can't sit still or pay attention certainly can disrupt a class and make teaching difficult. Then the teachers' and peers' reactions to the disruption can breed anger, anxiety, depression, and poor self-esteem, among other problems. In short order, the child develops multiple sources of difficulty, and as time goes on, the list can keep getting longer.

One way of looking at the problem is to consider the child's temperament and how it fits with his environment. A person's temperament is his inborn personality and behavioral characteristics, including his activity level, attention span, stubbornness, adaptability, intensity, impulsivity, emotionality (moodiness), sociability, and responsiveness to various types of sensory stimulation. Our society, and particularly our schools, clearly value certain temperamental characteristics over others. For example, a child who has a long attention span, adapts easily to new situations, and has a pleasant, sunny mood will undoubtedly fit into the school environment more harmoniously than will a child who has a short attention span, has difficulty adjusting to changes, and seems grumpy or unhappy much of the time. Children with ADHD have particular trouble fitting into what society deems as normal or acceptable.

Some temperament researchers argue that such children do fall within the broad spectrum of normalcy and that no such disorder as ADHD truly exists, but even the most ardent critics acknowledge that some children, whether labeled "ADHD" or not, whether considered "normal" or "abnormal," have problems functioning effectively in their environment and that these children can be helped with appropriate interventions.

The diagnosis of ADHD, then, is more or less a convenient and logical way to approach a child's problem. But in terms of how to help the child with the difficulties associated with ADHD, the precision of the label is less important than determining where his functioning is most impaired. Many children who come to psychologists' or pediatricians' offices for treatment of behavioral problems or school difficulties are laden with bags full of symptoms. Typically, the question on their parents' minds is "Does my child have ADHD?" While the answer may be imprecise, asking the question can be worthwhile if it leads to an evaluation of the source and severity of the child's problems and indicates a set of possible interventions.

THE CORE SYMPTOMS

In the American Psychiatric Association's (APA) latest *Diagnostic and Statistical Manual of Mental Disorders (DSM-III-R)*, fourteen behavioral characteristics, or symptoms, are listed for ADHD. To qualify for a diagnosis of ADHD, a child must exhibit eight of these characteristics (see box). Further, the symptoms must have appeared before the age of seven and existed for longer than six months. Other possible causes of hyperactivity or inattention, such as a reaction to medication or some particularly stressful situation, must be ruled out.

Diagnostic criteria for 314.01 Attention-deficit Hyperactivity Disorder

Note: Consider a criterion met only if the behavior is considerably more frequent than that of most people of the same mental age.

A. A disturbance of at least six months during which at least eight of the following are present:

1   often fidgets with hands or feet or squirms in seat (in adolescents, may be limited to subjective feelings of restlessness)
2   has difficulty remaining seated when required to do so
3   is easily distracted by extraneous stimuli
4   has difficulty awaiting turn in games or group situations
5   often blurts out answers to questions before they have been completed
6   has difficulty following through on instructions from others (not due to oppositional behavior or failure of comprehension), e.g., fails to finish chores
7   has difficulty sustaining attention in tasks or play activities
8   often shifts from one uncompleted activity to another
9   has difficulty playing quietly
10 often talks excessively
11 often interrupts or intrudes on others, e.g., butts into other children's games
12 often does not seem to listen to what is being said to him or her
13 often loses things necessary for tasks or activities at school or at home (e.g., toys, pencils, books, assignments)
14 often engages in physically dangerous activities without considering possible consequences (not for the purpose of thrill-seeking), e.g., runs into street without looking

Note: The above items are listed in descending order of discriminating power based on data from a national field trial of the DSM-III-R criteria for Disruptive Behavior Disorders.

B. Onset before the age of seven.

C. Does not meet the criteria for a Pervasive Developmental Disorder.

Criteria for severity of Attention-deficit Hyperactivity Disorder:

Mild: Few, if any, symptoms in excess of those required to make the diagnosis **and** only minimal or no impairment in school and social functioning.

Moderate: Symptoms or functional impairment intermediate between "mild" and "severe."

Severe: Many symptoms in excess of those required to make the diagnosis and significant and pervasive impairment in functioning at home and school and with peers.

These fourteen characteristics, taken together, describe a child who is inattentive, impulsive, and/or hyperactive. These three characteristics are said to be the "core symptoms" of ADHD. A child need not display all core symptoms; that is, he may be inattentive but not hyperactive. But according to the APA guidelines, he must meet eight of the fourteen criteria for a diagnosis. Further, each of these criteria must be viewed in terms of what is considered "developmentally appropriate" for the child's chronological age. For example, a three-year-old shouldn't be expected to sit still for twenty minutes, whereas a nine-year-old should.

According to the APA guidelines, a child may be considered "mild" if he exhibits only eight of these symptoms and is only mildly impaired from functioning effectively in his environment. Having nine to ten of the symptoms warrants a "moderate" tag, and having more than eleven symptoms constitutes a "severe" case. A child with severe ADHD is one who has multiple areas of significant difficulty. In addition to the fourteen criteria listed in *DSM-III-R* there are other factors—intensity, persistence, and resistance to therapy—that must be considered when deciding whether a child is mildly, moderately, or severely affected. For example, a child who is so impulsive that he frequently puts himself in danger might warrant a "severe" classification, even though he exhibits only eight or nine of the diagnostic criteria. Another child may be so unresponsive to environmental manipulations that although he exhibits few of the criteria, his level of functioning is drastically affected.

Chapter 2 discusses the history of how this list of symptoms came to be written. Suffice it to say here that there is nothing either magical or absolute about it. The list is simply a tool that can help identify children who may fit into the broad classification of ADHD. These diagnostic guidelines have many weaknesses. They do not specify who should decide whether a child exhibits these behaviors; they do not provide objective measures of symptoms, and they do not define "age-appropriate." Thus, the ADHD diagnosis still remains open to various interpretations and opinions. Moreover, you should note that the list refers only to behaviors—it says nothing about intelligence or personality. The fact is that ADHD is defined in terms of behavior, even though your child is much more than a list of behaviors.

INATTENTION, DISTRACTIBILITY *Inattentiveness* is characteristic of a child who doesn't pay attention for a reasonable length of time. He may daydream or be easily distracted. He has difficulty concentrating on schoolwork or other activities that require sustained attention, and he therefore has trouble completing tasks. He has trouble following through on instructions, especially if they involve multiple steps. He appears not to listen. He often loses or forgets things.

Surprisingly, many children who are said to be inattentive show a remarkable ability to pay attention under certain circumstances—for example, while watching TV or playing video games. In addition, many children attend well when they are in a doctor's office or when they are interacting one-to-one with an adult. Their ability to pay attention only at certain times can actually add to such children's problems. Parents and teachers may interpret their selective attention as an indication that they are simply not trying to pay attention sometimes. A doctor may conclude from his observation of the child in his office that no such inattentiveness exists—that the parent is overreacting or, worse, precipitating the bad behavior.

IMPULSIVITY *Impulsivity* refers to the process of acting before one thinks. The impulsive child may blurt out in class, interrupt the teacher, or bother other students. He has trouble waiting for his turn. He has difficulty planning his actions and often shows poor judgment. He may put himself in dangerous situations, such as by running out into the street before looking for cars. He may also have difficulty controlling antisocial impulses, such as stealing and lying.

HYPERACTIVITY *Hyperactivity* means different things for children of different ages. Generally, hyperactive children seem to be always on the go and unable to sit still. They may fidget or squirm excessively, talk constantly, and have trouble playing quietly.

OTHER CORE SYMPTOMS Other temperamental and behavioral characteristics that are not included on the *DSM-III-R* list may actually go more to the heart of what constitutes ADHD than those that are included. Many ADHD children have frequent *mood swings*—what is called "emotional lability" in the terminology of professionals. They have a low threshold for becoming *emotionally overaroused* and thus frequently have a *low frustration tolerance* and a *hot temper.* They can be extremely *demanding of one's attention,* frequently acting the part of the class clown or displaying annoying attention-getting behaviors. They may have *difficulty adjusting to new situations* and have *a hard time following rules.* In addition, many are *poorly motivated* and *lack a desire to please* teachers or parents.

ASSOCIATED PROBLEMS

All these temperamental and behavioral characteristics can be thought of as "core symptoms" when they are central to what creates difficulties in a child's life. But relatively few children exhibit only these core symptoms. Most experience one or more associated problems, such as learning disabilities, oppositional behaviors, conduct disorders, mood disorders, or anxiety disorders. It is not always easy to separate the various problems a child may be having, since each problem influences and interacts with the others, and the relative importance of any one problem may change over time. For example, if a child is inattentive, has learning difficulties, and is anxious, it may be difficult to tell if his anxiety arises from his learning difficulties and if they, in turn, arise from his inattentiveness. Or is he primarily an anxious child whose inattentiveness and learning difficulties arise from his anxiety? In either case, all three problems must be dealt with. The purpose of diagnosis is to identify which of the problems are most important and which are amenable to treatment. Sometimes the course of management involves peeling at the layers, dealing with one problem first before tackling the others.

LEARNING DISABILITIES The incidence of identifiable learning disabilities among children with ADHD may be as high as 30 to 40 percent, according to some researchers. This probably represents only the tip of the iceberg; most children with ADHD have some learning problems. In fact, school difficulties are almost universal among ADHD children, and they are often the main reason that children are referred for treatment.

In assessing a child's learning difficulties, it is important to determine whether the child has a specific learning disability or if other problems are impairing his ability to learn. For instance, inattention, distractibility, impulsivity, low frustration tolerance, and moodiness can all lead to *learning difficulties*. By contrast, a *learning disability* is a more intrinsic developmental weakness that affects a child's ability to learn. A specific learning disability may, in turn, lead the child to become frustrated, inattentive, distractible, and so on. When a child exhibits the symptoms of ADHD and has learning difficulties as well, it is often hard to determine which is the primary problem; that is, whether the child's attentional or other behavioral problems lead to his learning difficulties, or whether a specific learning disability leads to his restlessness, impulsivity, and inattention as secondary problems. A major goal of diagnostic assessment is to sort out the two so that intervention can be designed appropriately (see chapter 6).

The learning-disabled child is one who has trouble in one or more areas of learning because of some difference in the way his or her brain receives or processes information. A learning disability does not indicate low intelligence—to the contrary, only children with at least average or near-average intelligence can be said to be learning disabled. (Children with well-below-average intelligence are said to be mildly to severely mentally retarded.) In fact, learning-disabled children may be of high or even superior intelligence. A learning disability may affect a child's ability to perceive, integrate, remember, or express information. It often becomes apparent in the early years of elementary school, when the child's performance in school lags behind his innate or perceived ability.

Learning disabilities can affect many different facets of the learning process. Some learning-disabled children have trouble with visual or auditory perception. Others have difficulty understanding or organizing the information they receive. Some have memory disabilities. And others have trouble communicating, either because of language problems or because of motor difficulties that affect their ability to write.

Some learning disabilities mimic attention deficit disorders. For example, a child who doesn't ever seem to listen may appear to be inattentive, but in actuality he may be unable to focus in on or "hear" what is being said. That child might have an *auditory perception disability,* which makes it difficult for him to hear subtle differences in sounds. He may confuse the words you are saying, or he may not be able to pick out your voice over other sounds in the environment.

Learning disabilities often become apparent in schoolchildren with ADHD when they begin to have difficulty with verbal activities, including reading and/or writing. Other children with symptoms of ADHD may be identified as having nonverbal learning disabilities. Nonverbal disabilities affect visual perception, visual-motor function (in tasks such as writing), and the organization of visual information. Children with nonverbal learning disabilities tend to be disorganized and inattentive, and they are frequently more socially withdrawn and anxious than other learning-disabled children. But since they often can read and do mathematics adequately, their learning disability may go undetected and untreated. Their difficulties may be attributed instead to inattentiveness, distractibility, or lack of motivation. This cluster of symptoms, it should be noted, may represent a rather unique subset of children with ADHD.

Whatever kind of learning disability a child has, it can either lead to frustration and inattentiveness or it can be masked by more prominent inattentive and hyperactive behavior. The two problems—learning disability and attention deficits—are so intertwined that some researchers believe they are two sides of the same coin; that is, that a learning disability is the cognitive aspect of a problem and the attention deficit disorder the behavioral aspect of the same problem. No matter which is the more basic or severe, most children need attention for both their learning and their behavioral problems. Learning difficulties cannot be adequately addressed when a child cannot pay attention. And if a learning disability is contributing to a child's inattention, addressing the learning disability can help alleviate the inattentiveness.

CONDUCT DISORDERS AND OPPOSITIONAL BEHAVIOR Many children diagnosed with ADHD show some oppositional behavior—refusing to comply with parents' or teachers' requests, procrastinating, throwing temper tantrums, and generally being defiant with adults. These children may be labeled as having an *oppositional disorder* if their defiant behavior becomes problematic. A more serious problem arises when a child shows antisocial behavior with his peers; for instance, if he is aggressive or steals. This more severe behavior may warrant a diagnosis of *conduct disorder.* According to the *DSM-III-R,* the core symptom of a conduct disorder is a violation of the basic rights of others or of major societal norms. The overlap of conduct disorders with ADHD is quite high; one-third to one-half of children who have a conduct disorder also have ADHD. These children are more impulsive, more physically and verbally aggressive, more hostile, and less empathic than ADHD children without a conduct disorder. They may lie, steal, fight, set fires, and run away. Conduct-disordered children are at high risk for having long-term problems, including juvenile delinquency, sociopathy, alcoholism, and substance abuse.

While a child with a conduct disorder is at high risk for future problems, the same cannot be said for a child with defiant or oppositional behavior. Oppositional children are not simply in the early stages of a conduct disorder and are not necessarily headed for trouble.

MOOD DISORDERS Mood disorders include depression, dysthymia, and occasionally bipolar disorder (more commonly known as manic-depressive illness). In adults, *depression* is characterized by sadness, fatigue, feelings of worthlessness, and insomnia, among other features. In children and adolescents, depression may appear as irritability. In both children and adults, depression can cause a loss of concentration, which may look like inattentiveness.

Dysthymia is less severe than depression. It appears as a chronic state of low self-esteem and negative feelings about one's own abilities. People with *bipolar disorder* experience alternating periods of depression and mania. During the manic period, a person may appear hyperactive and distractible. Bipolar disorder is rarely diagnosed in children. When a child has a mood disorder in addition to ADHD, his problems can become magnified. But again, it can be difficult to separate the two problems.

ANXIETY DISORDERS In children, three major anxiety disorders may either coexist with or mimic ADHD: overanxious disorder of childhood, separation-anxiety disorder, and post-traumatic stress disorder. Generally, anxious children are extremely tense and self-conscious and unusually and unrealistically fearful and worried; they may exhibit physical symptoms such as stomachaches or headaches. Children who harbor excessive worry about the future or concerns about past behaviors may be said to be *overanxious*. Those who become extremely anxious when faced with separation from an important person or object in their life may be said to suffer from *separation-anxiety disorder*. Separation reactions are common in young children, but when they persist past early childhood, they may indicate an anxiety disorder. *Post-traumatic stress disorder* may arise as a result of separation, loss, injury, abuse, or some other traumatic event in the child's life.

Anxiety disorders often are difficult to recognize because they overlap with so many other problematic behaviors. For example, anxiety often intermingles with depression, inattentiveness, and distractibility. Depression, inattentiveness, and distractibility may lead to anxiety, or anxiety can result in inattentiveness and distractibility. Treating the attentional problem or the depression will sometimes relieve the anxiety, while at other times anxiety is the primary problem and complicates the treatment of ADHD or depression.

OTHER ASSOCIATED DIFFICULTIES

Children, adolescents, and adults with ADHD may manifest still other difficulties that can complicate treatment or influence outcome.

PERSONALITY DISORDERS Personality disorders are not diagnosed in children because, by definition, they can appear only after the personality is fully formed, which occurs sometime during adolescence. The personality disorder most commonly associated with ADHD is *antisocial personality*. Children with conduct disorders have a high likelihood of developing an antisocial personality during adolescence. A person with an antisocial personality is one likely to engage in criminal behaviors, such as stealing, with no sense of guilt.

SUBSTANCE ABUSE   Substance abuse often accompanies many of the other problems listed here, including ADHD. But again, it is often difficult to determine which problem came first. For example, sometimes substance abuse arises as a result of un-treated ADHD, as people seek an escape from their over-whelming difficulties. For others, substance abuse results when people try to medicate themselves for their own unrec-ognized ADHD-like behaviors, as some doctors have sug-gested. Substance abuse also overlaps extensively with antiso-cial personality, although some substance abusers get into antisocial behaviors only as a way of supporting their addic-tion.

COORDINATION PROBLEMS   About half of all children diagnosed with ADHD also have coordination problems that affect ei-ther their fine or their gross motor skills. They may have poor eye-hand coordination or simply appear clumsy and un-coordinated. While this is neither a behavioral nor an intel-lectual disability, it can add to the problems of ADHD chil-dren, especially boys. Other children may tease and ridicule them and ostracize them from their games and sports. Con-versely, athletic talent can go a long way toward compensat-ing for poor social skills—again, particularly for boys.

TIC DISORDERS AND TOURETTE SYNDROME   Some children with ADHD also have tic disorders, ranging from mild eye twitches to more complex jerking, jumping, or skipping movements. Tics may also be vocal in nature, ranging from repetitive throat clearing or grunting to the involuntary use of obscenities. Many if not most people experience mild, transient tics at some time in their lives. Fewer people de-velop chronic motor tics. The most severe tic disorder is called Tourette syndrome and involves multiple motor as well as vocal tics that last for more than a year. Some 40 to 60 percent of children with tic disorders also have ADHD, although only about 20 percent of children with ADHD also have tic disorders. Usually, these tic disorders are mild; only a few percent of children with ADHD also have full-blown

Tourette syndrome. Many researchers suspect that both ADHD and tic disorders arise from the same neurochemical imbalance. Tics generally appear between the ages of seven and ten, several years after the symptoms associated with ADHD become apparent. They may worsen, however, when Ritalin or other stimulant medication is taken.

OTHER PSYCHIATRIC CONDITIONS Other psychiatric conditions such as phobias (excessive fearfulness), eating disorders, and obsessive-compulsive disorder may also be present with ADHD. *Obsessive-compulsive disorder,* or OCD, is a type of anxiety disorder in which affected people become obsessively focused on some aspect of their lives, such as cleanliness. Obsessive and compulsive behavior usually does not appear until the teenage years. Younger children with OCD may display ADHD-like behaviors of inattentiveness and distractibility. OCD occurs in nearly two-thirds of patients with Tourette syndrome, which has led to the suspicion that they are linked, or possibly different manifestations of the same underlying problem. Some researchers speculate that OCD reflects the conscious and voluntary aspects and Tourette Syndrome the unconscious and involuntary aspects of a similar neurological dysfunction.

Patients who have undiagnosed ADHD that has led to depression and frustration may ultimately develop an *eating disorder* as a result. The most common phobias seen in children, whether they have ADHD or not, are fear of separation or darkness. Most children outgrow these while still young. Some children fear and avoid social situations. As young children, they may be labeled "avoidant." Later, if the problem is not addressed, they may develop a more serious "social phobia," which virtually paralyzes them from interacting with other people. Though avoidant disorder/social phobia can occur in any child, it is seen with greater frequency among children with ADHD, and in fact may represent a separate cluster of children with ADHD.

OTHER CONDITIONS THAT MAY COEXIST WITH **ADHD**

ADHD is often seen in children who have seizure disorders or mental retardation. In either case, the attentional problems may result from the same brain injury that led to the seizures or retardation (see chapter 3). Or in the case of patients with seizure disorders, the ADHD symptoms may arise as a side effect of anticonvulsant medication, which can precipitate or aggravate the symptoms of ADHD. In addition, some children who are suspected of having ADHD turn out to be experiencing mild types of seizures that appear as inattention. For these children, treatment of the seizure disorder may eliminate the ADHD-like symptoms.

For a mentally retarded child to be diagnosed with ADHD, his symptoms of inattention, impulsivity, and hyperactivity must be considered inappropriate for his mental or developmental rather than chronological age.

SECONDARY PROBLEMS Whatever constellation of difficulties an ADHD child has, they can work synergistically to create multiple problems, including underachievement, depression, low motivation, and poor self-esteem. The nature and intensity of the problems of an individual child depend on the interplay of the symptoms and their severity. To illustrate this variability, consider Eliot and Sam (see box).

THE CHANGING FACE OF **ADHD**

The cases of Eliot and Sam illustrate not only that ADHD varies from child to child but that it varies depending on a child's age. Sam, at five, is thought of as "immature" by his teachers. His difficulties are primarily behavioral and are not related to either cognitive abilities or emotional problems. Fifteen-year-old Eliot, however, has multiple problems— ADHD, tics, dysthymia, and conduct disorder. Frustration and anger have built up in Eliot for nearly ten years, bringing him to the breaking point. He has spoken of suicide and has been hospitalized for several weeks. Eliot is an extreme ex-

Eliot

Eliot is fifteen and has been treated for ADHD since he was six. By the age of seven he had developed serious tics—facial blinks and grimaces that he cannot control. Though he is quite bright, his inattentiveness and hyperactivity have led to academic problems. Moreover, he is constantly teased about his tics. Not surprisingly, he feels like a failure. He is angry at his schoolmates and is depressed much of the time. His behavior has deteriorated to the point that he has been kicked out of school several times.

Sam

Sam is a five-year-old child who doesn't seem to listen or hear when he is spoken to. He blurts out in class, has trouble sitting still, and won't wait his turn. In kindergarten, his teachers spend a large part of the day responding to his antics, repeating instructions over and over just for him, and disciplining him when he breaks the rules. Sometimes they just try to ignore him. The other children know that Sam is the "bad boy" in the class. They avoid him because he won't share and because he tends to play too roughly for many of them. While the other children are working on reading-readiness skills, Sam often wanders off to the play area, and his teachers are only too happy to have him out of the way.

Though he is only five and has only moderate ADHD, Sam is at risk for school failure both because of his inattentiveness and because his teachers allow him to avoid schoolwork so that they can avoid hassles. He is already showing signs of poor self-esteem; sometimes he thinks of himself as "bad" and worries because the other children don't like him. He tries to get attention by clowning around and sometimes by pushing or hitting the other children, but both of those behaviors elicit even more punishment and ostracization from his teachers and friends.

ample of how an ADHD child's difficulties can build up over time.

Although ADHD is thought to be inborn, most often it is not diagnosed before age five or six. Several factors can help explain why this is so. First, the symptoms of ADHD are developmentally inappropriate behaviors—for instance, an activity level in a nine-year-old that would be more typical of a six- or seven-year-old. In young children, however, the abnormalities of any of the core symptoms are hardly noticeable unless they are severe. Inattentiveness is not likely to be apparent in the early years because few demands are usually placed on young children's attention spans. Hyperactivity and impulsivity are so commonly seen in young children that abnormalities are unlikely to stand out unless they are extreme.

The second reason that ADHD is rarely diagnosed in young children is that most often the behaviors become problematic only when a child confronts the structure of school. At home, many parents adjust the environment so that it fits the child's temperament. Frequently, such parents are not even aware that they have made those adjustments. They may accept hyperactive behavior with the thought "Boys will be boys" and proceed to modify their home so that the child harms neither himself nor the living space. Furthermore, few new parents have much experience with what constitutes normal and overactive behavior in a young child. When such parents are told by a teacher that their child is unusually overactive, they often reflect back and say, "Yes, he's always been like that; but I thought all little children acted that way."

Still another factor that contributes to the low frequency of preschool diagnoses is the tremendous variability in normal behavior among young children. At age three, many children have seemingly endless amounts of energy, and nearly all these children are normal. By age six or seven, however, children display less variability, and the overactive child stands out as different from the others.

Nevertheless, some children *are* diagnosed and treated before the age of five. They tend to be children who are extremely overactive. When looking back on the early years of children who are later diagnosed as having ADHD, a picture emerges of the young ADHD child. (Keep in mind, however, that no two children with ADHD are exactly alike and that neither the presence nor absence of any of these behavioral characteristics tells whether a child has ADHD.)

As infants, ADHD children may be extremely fussy or colicky. Some have poor eating or sleeping habits. They are often very active or even physically precocious—pulling up to a stand, climbing out of the crib, and walking or running earlier than expected. For example, Danny, whom we met in the introduction, was described as a "tornado" by his mother. Generally, activity levels increase until about the age of three, but then they begin to decrease somewhat. By the time the child reaches adolescence, overactivity frequently has ceased to be a problem.

As the baby reaches his preschool years, his overactivity, short attention span, low frustration tolerance, and difficulty adjusting to new situations begin to create problems for him in getting along with other children. These problems follow him into elementary school and are exacerbated by his difficulties functioning appropriately in the classroom. He is often disruptive, noncooperative, and unable to follow classroom rules. If he has a learning disability on top of his attentional problems, he may become increasingly frustrated. As the elementary school years go by, the demands placed on his attention increase and he begins to do increasingly poorly academically. He may also begin to show signs of poor self-esteem, depression, and mounting frustration.

Adolescence presents a new set of challenges. In years past, it was thought that ADHD disappeared when a child reached puberty. This is no longer thought to be true. Although overactivity may diminish with time, inattention and impulsivity often persist and can be compounded by past failures, a low sense of self-esteem, and the other stresses of adolescence. Antisocial behavior may become prominent at this time.

GIRLS WITH ADHD

All these characteristics can apply to either boys or girls. But according to some researchers, girls with ADHD often display a slightly different constellation of difficulties. They tend to be more anxious and have more severe cognitive deficits. At the same time, they tend to be less hyperactive, less physically aggressive, and less likely to lose their tempers. Since aggression is often the characteristic that brings children to treatment, some girls with ADHD and with the potential for developing school problems, low self-esteem, and emotional difficulties may go undetected.

SUBTYPING

The wide variability in the behavior of children with behavioral problems presents many dilemmas for physicians, child psychiatrists, psychologists, and parents who are trying to determine whether ADHD is an appropriate diagnosis for an individual child. It also presents dilemmas for researchers trying to make some sense of the field. Many attempts have been made to identify subtypes of ADHD, in the hope that classifying children according to subtype would allow researchers to work with more homogeneous groups of children and therefore lead to clearer and more definitive information. In addition, it is hoped, subtyping could lead to treatments that are more specifically matched to a child's particular array of symptoms.

Unfortunately, there is no universal agreement about subtyping. Nevertheless, a few groups of children do manifest symptoms of ADHD and have certain other specific characteristics as well that require special attention. This has given rise to several loose classifications.

ATTENTION DEFICITS WITHOUT HYPERACTIVITY Some children diagnosed as having ADHD are not overactive. These children have created a conundrum for diagnosticians. Some feel that these children differ from other children with ADHD more than they resemble them and thus constitute a completely separate group. Although they come to the attention of parents and teachers for similar reasons—especially school failure—their "abnormal" behaviors tend to be internalizing rather than externalizing. In other words, they tend to be more sluggish, anxious, and shy, and less impulsive, distractible, and aggressive. Fewer of these children are diagnosed as having conduct disorders, and they are less likely to experience social rejection than hyperactive children with ADHD. Because they are not hyperactive, they may not be considered as having ADHD at all. Consequently, they are often faulted for not trying and are at high risk for academic trouble and poor self-concept. Recent research also suggests that they are poor responders to psychostimulant medications. Thus, even if they are diagnosed as having ADHD, the standard treatment may be ineffective.

ADHD AND THE MENTALLY GIFTED Children who have ADHD encompass the entire range of intelligence levels, including those who are considered "mentally gifted." In general, the higher a child's level of intelligence, the better his prognosis is because he can often use his intelligence to compensate for his other difficulties. But although "mentally gifted" children can succeed through great effort and intelligence, they may also be penalized because teachers fail to recognize their difficulties and may fault them for being poorly motivated. Such children tend to have problems with organization and may take longer to get things done. In addition, they tend to suffer greatly in the area of self-esteem because they are viewed as lazy underachievers, who "should" be able to shine academically.

EXPECTATIONS FOR CHILDREN WITH ADHD

As parents learn more about what it means for a child to be diagnosed as having ADHD and as they gain a greater understanding and appreciation for their child's difficulties, they may remain unsure about how much they can expect from him. For example, if a child is failing at a particular task, his parents may ask themselves whether it is because he *can't* do it or because he *won't* do it. In such situations, it is helpful to reframe the question to ask "Is it because he doesn't possess the necessary skills and knowledge or because he doesn't use the skills and knowledge successfully?" By reframing the question, parents can see that the two aspects are so interrelated that the answer is "both." Even if a child's problem is in using the skills he has, that problem prevents him from acquiring new skills, and thus his difficulties spiral.

Accordingly, parents of children with ADHD must rethink their expectations. For example, it may be unwise to expect a child with ADHD to complete a complex school report on his own. But with some guidance and over time, the child can learn to accommodate his difficulties so that he can achieve success, though possibly through a different route from the one most of the children in his class follow. Likewise, a child may have difficulty playing football, which requires a high degree of focus, attention, and teamwork, but he may shine at another sport, such as tennis, that requires other qualities.

Joel is a successful doctor who is able to juggle his practice, research, and administrative duties with a great deal of energy. But he was not always this way. As a child, he could not sit still and was constantly thrown out of class because he was so disruptive. He could never remember what he was supposed to do or what commitments he had made. Over time he learned coping skills. He learned that he had to put extraordinary amounts of effort into organizing his activities; everything had to be written down and scheduled, and he had to complete one thing before he could move on to the next. He taught himself these skills and strategies through trial and error, aggravation, and many failures, but they saw him through college and medical school and continue to fuel his success as an adult.

Although his ADHD created many problems for Joel, it may also have worked to his advantage. As an adult, his high energy level and quick thinking ability may be ADHD-related characteristics that have contributed to his success. As Joel's story illustrates, a person with ADHD can accomplish many things. But in order to do so, he must learn to adjust to and work around his limitations. Your job as a parent is to help your child find his way—to guide him to the appropriate treatments and activities that will allow him to grow up feeling successful, in control of himself, and worthwhile. It is not an easy task, but it can be done.

CHAPTER 2

A Historical Perspective

The disorder that we call ADHD today has a written history that goes back to the turn of the century. At that time, behavioral problems were associated with brain damage. Thinking about the disorder has evolved over time as scientists have tried to identify its essential components, causes, and prevalence. Many questions about ADHD remain far from being resolved, but a glimpse into the past can help put today's controversy into perspective.

Some medical mysteries are solved through a process of elimination; that is, first a wide number of possibilities are considered and one by one are systematically excluded as the central problem becomes clearer. The study of ADHD has not followed this course; rather, researchers have moved from a narrowly defined conception of the disorder—that is, as behavioral difficulties arising from brain damage—to a broader notion that includes multiple possible causes and modes of treatment. The existence of a single, simple explanation no longer appears reasonable, and correspondingly, the application of a single, specific drug treatment no longer seems appropriate.

For people with ADHD and for parents of children with ADHD, this means that a simple solution is unlikely to be effective. But as solutions have become more complex, they have also become better designed to address the total needs of children with ADHD and their families.

THE EARLY FOCUS ON BRAIN INJURY

In 1902, Dr. George F. Still said that children he had treated who were impulsive, hyperactive, inattentive, and trouble-makers were suffering from defects in moral control, and he attributed their problems to organic disorders of the brain. Over the next three decades, other researchers associated similar behaviors with specific forms of brain injury. They noted that children who had contracted encephalitis, a viral infection of the nervous system, during an encephalitis outbreak after World War I displayed a high incidence of hyperactivity, impulsivity, and conduct disorders. In the 1940s, behavioral disturbances were observed in soldiers who had suffered brain injuries. These observations seemed to support the assumption that brain damage led to behavioral problems. In fact, this association between brain damage and behavioral problems remains accepted today.

But these observations also led to a conclusion that turned out to be erroneous. Some scientists suggested that if brain damage led to these characteristic behavioral problems, then the presence of such behavioral problems indicated that the child had suffered brain damage. No such brain damage was apparent in most of these children, so the damage was assumed to be mild and thus undetectable. Hyperactive children were said to suffer from "minimal brain damage" or "minimal brain dysfunction," even though the presence of even minimal damage was and remains unproven. In the late 1950s, this concept was reinforced when a study of children with behavioral problems revealed that their mothers had suffered more complications of pregnancy than had the mothers of children without behavioral problems. Again, brain damage—this time, thought to have occurred prenatally—was blamed.

Meanwhile, in 1937, Charles Bradley reported that he had successfully intervened with hyperactive children using the central nervous system stimulant Benzedrine. Fifty percent of the children who were given Benzedrine in his study showed a reduction in hyperactivity and an improvement in attention span and impulse control. Bradley's research further supported the idea that behavioral problems were indicative of an organic or neurological deficit. Another stimulant medication, Ritalin (methylphenidate), was first used in 1959, and by the mid-1960s it was widely used as a treatment for what was then known as hyperkinesis, minimal brain dysfunction, or any of a dozen other names.

ATTEMPTS AT CONSISTENCY

In 1966, the U.S. Department of Health, Education, and Welfare established a task force to try to clarify the terminology surrounding the disorder. By that time, the disorder was being widely diagnosed in schools throughout the country. The governmental agency settled on the name *minimal brain dysfunction,* or MBD. Children with MBD were said to be of near-average to above-average intelligence and to have learning or behavioral disabilities caused by functional disturbances of the central nervous system.

Acceptance of the name *minimal brain dysfunction* was short-lived. In 1968, the APA revised its standard diagnostic manual, the *Diagnostic and Statistical Manual of Mental Disorders,* and this second edition *(DSM-II)* included "hyperkinetic disorder of childhood" as a valid diagnostic category for the first time. Before this, the *DSM* had barely addressed children's psychiatric problems. *DSM-II* described the hyperkinetic child as characterized by a short attention span, restlessness, and overactivity, but it gave no guidelines for diagnosis.

In fact, diagnostic tools for hyperkinetic children were in their infancy at the time *DSM-II* was written. Psychologist C. Keith Conners had developed a rating scale for teachers that he used to evaluate children's responses to treatment. The

Conners Teacher Rating Scale (CTRS) was the first standardized instrument available, and it remains, in a revised form, a widely used tool for the diagnosis of ADHD today. In its original form, the CTRS listed thirty-nine behaviors and asked teachers to note whether the child exhibited each behavior "not at all," "just a little," "pretty much," or "very much." These answers were rated on a scale from zero ("not at all") to three ("very much"). Using Conners' scale, researchers identified children who scored significantly higher than the majority of children—that is, they were extreme relative to their peers. This scoring system soon became the standard tool used by researchers and clinicians for identifying hyperkinetic children.

The CTRS was not based on any data that showed that the behaviors Conners had chosen were, in fact, indicative of hyperactivity. Nevertheless, the scale established, for the first time, a tool that yielded a somewhat objective measure of children's behavior. Moreover, by focusing attention on children's behavior in school, the scale suggested that hyperactivity, inattention, and impulsivity were school-based problems and that in order to fully understand and treat them, the classroom had to be considered.

The focus on schools heightened in 1970, when *The Washington Post* reported on a study that had revealed that 5 to 10 percent of the children enrolled in the Omaha public schools were being given drugs, primarily Ritalin, to "improve classroom deportment and increase learning potential."[1] The report suggested that the children were being drugged into quiet submission for the convenience of teachers, who naturally reported that they had less trouble in controlling disruptive behavior. The report was later discredited as being a misinterpretation of the data, but this "Omaha incident" and a subsequent book called *The Myth of the Hyperactive Child*[2] continue to have a pervasive effect on the field, scaring parents, doctors, and teachers alike. In recent years, the Ritalin controversy has been given new life through a number of lawsuits that claim that Ritalin drugs children into passivity and causes suicide, psychosis, and depression. Nevertheless, despite all the controversy (and for reasons described in chapter 6), Ritalin remains the mainstay of treatment for behavioral problems manifested by inattentiveness and/or hyperactivity.

THE FOCUS ON ATTENTION AND HYPERACTIVITY

Throughout this period, researchers continued to try to clarify the constellation of behaviors that characterized the so-called hyperactive or hyperkinetic child. Studies by Virginia Douglas and her colleagues at McGill University focused on inattention as the central problem common to all these children. Unlike overactivity, which seemed to diminish with time, two aspects of attentional difficulty—sustaining attention and maintaining impulse control—appeared to last throughout childhood and possibly into adulthood. Douglas's research suggested that the disorder was characterized by multiple deficits, including subtle cognitive deficiencies, rather than by one central problem of hyperactivity. This research led to another revision of the *DSM* in 1980 that reflected the multifaceted nature of the problem.

DSM-III provided the first detailed description of the disorder and renamed it attention deficit disorder with hyperactivity (ADDH). Moreover, *DSM-III* proposed that the condition could exist in the absence of hyperactivity. *DSM-III* established three categories of behavior that constituted a diagnosis of ADDH: inattention, impulsivity, and hyperactivity. For each of these categories, five or six "symptoms" were listed. In order to garner a diagnosis of ADDH, a child had to display two or three symptoms in all three categories; a diagnosis of ADD without hyperactivity would be given to a child who displayed symptoms listed under inattention and impulsivity but not hyperactivity.

DSM-III brought order and consistency to the diagnosis of

attention deficit disorders, but its criteria were questioned. Furthermore, its distinctions between the three categories of symptoms lacked clarity. For example, although the behavior "has difficulty sticking to a play activity" was listed as a symptom of inattention, the same behavior can also reflect impulsivity. Many people questioned whether the three categories truly represented three different aspects of a child's behavior or were simply different ways of looking at one basic behavioral characteristic.

The diagnostic criteria were further revised in 1987, when the APA published *DSM-III-R. DSM-III-R* eliminated the three categories of symptoms and lumped all the symptoms into one list, as we have seen in chapter 1. In addition, the revision threw out the terminology *ADDH with or without hyperactivity* and replaced it with the name *attention deficit–hyperactivity disorder,* or *ADHD.* This change marked a subtle shift in emphasis toward considering both inattention and hyperactivity as important characteristics of the disorder. *DSM-III-R* listed fourteen symptoms and required that a child meet eight of them to qualify for a diagnosis of ADHD. The revision also established a new diagnostic category for children who would have been diagnosed as ADD without hyperactivity under the old criteria but who did not quite meet the criteria for ADHD under the new guidelines. Such children may now receive a diagnosis of undifferentiated ADD (UADD).

Although *DSM-III-R* was another attempt to clarify the disorder, it too is much criticized. Some clinicians and researchers argue that the multifaceted definition prescribed in *DSM-III* is more appropriate than the unidimensional definition in *DSM-III-R.* By lumping all the symptom clusters (inattention, hyperactivity, and impulsivity) into one group, they maintain, *DSM-III-R* obscures distinctions among subtypes. Others hold that consistent and strong evidence is lacking that either list of symptoms accurately portrays a child with attention deficit disorder. Both lists were arrived at through a process of consensus, based on varying data sets accumulated by different groups of scientists measuring different characteristics with different tools. For *DSM-III-R,* the symptoms list was field tested and the items are listed in the order by which they differentiate a child with ADHD from a normal child. However, *DSM-III-R* does not specify the criteria to be used for identifying symptoms. It does not say whether information should be gathered from parents, teachers, or both, or which of the standard rating scales should be used, if any. Finally, the *DSM-III-R* list closely resembles the current Conners Teacher Rating Scale, which has been criticized because it includes items related to aggression in addition to those associated with ADHD. Thus, it may identify a more heterogeneous group of children, including ones with both aggressive disorders and ADHD. No one sees *DSM-III-R* as the final word on attention deficit disorders. Rather, it is regarded as one step toward a more rational approach. Researchers are already looking ahead to 1992, when *DSM-IV* is expected to be published. In the meantime, the terms *ADD* and *ADHD* are both commonly used.

In other parts of the world, still other classification systems have been devised. The World Health Organization's *International Classification of Disease (ICD)* is now in its tenth version. The *ICD* defines the syndrome it calls hyperkinesis more narrowly. It does not mention inattention, and it considers aggression and conduct disorders as different categories. Thus, many fewer children are identified as hyperkinetic under the *ICD* system. Many children who would be classified as ADHD in the United States would receive a diagnosis of conduct disorder in Britain.

How Common Is ADHD?

Incidence estimates for ADHD vary widely, depending on who is doing the measuring, what tools they are using to assess incidence, and where they are doing it. Studies done in the Isle of Wight, for example, where the *ICD* criteria are used, have suggested an incidence of only 0.1 percent, while some studies in areas as geographically distant as Uganda and Canada have measured incidences as high as 23 percent. Even in studies done in the United States, incidence ranges from 1 percent to 20 percent. Most variation among these studies is probably due to the varying diagnostic tools (see chapter 5 for a description of these tools) and classification systems (*DSM* vs. *ICD,* for example) used and to the lack of objective measures of classification. For instance, some researchers relied on parent ratings; others relied on teacher ratings; and still others on ratings done by the researchers themselves. Some of the variation in incidence among different geographical areas may also be due to cultural or ethnic differences, although this has not been studied.

Based on the *DSM-III-R* criteria, it is reasonable to speculate that ADHD occurs in some 3 to 5 percent of the population of the U.S., which translates to as many as two million schoolchildren. The number of boys affected greatly exceeds the number of girls, probably by as much as six to one. As we have seen, however, some researchers believe that many girls with ADHD go undiagnosed because they are less overactive and disruptive and are therefore less likely to come to the attention of teachers.

In addition, for every child diagnosed with ADHD, there are probably another two or three who don't quite meet the criteria but who could benefit from some intervention. Many children who are struggling in school could be helped by medication, behavioral therapy, or some combination of treatments.

Many people believe that the incidence of ADHD is on the rise, owing to the fast pace and increasing pressures of Western society. Because the definition of the disorder and its diagnostic criteria have changed over the years, this belief is difficult to evaluate. If the disorder truly results from an inborn temperamental trait, the likelihood is that while incidence may not be changing with time, its manifestations are. In a highly technological society such as ours, the demands placed on people's time and attention are elevated to a point that some children with ADHD cannot reach. In the days of the Wild West, ADHD people may have been the men who served as scouts—they took off on their horses and rode over the next hill primarily because they couldn't sit still. But in today's world, attributes such as these are more problematic, and easy career paths for such individuals are harder to find.

CHAPTER 3

The Causes of Attention Deficits

When their child experiences behavioral or neurological problems, many parents run through a litany of questions—if not aloud, then at least in their minds: "Is it something I did wrong?" "Is it because I am an inadequate parent?" "Am I feeding him wrong?" "Has he been exposed to something noxious in the environment?"

The cause of ADHD remains unknown, but we do know that the answer to all these questions is usually no. Environmental factors, including parenting techniques, diet, and toxins, appear to affect the disorder, but they do not cause it. In most cases, the root of the problem lies in the child's genetic makeup.

In this chapter we will discuss the different factors that may play roles in the development of ADHD. The relative contribution of each factor varies from one child to the next. By developing an understanding of the root of your child's problem, you will have a clearer idea of what can be changed and what can't. We will also discuss the physiological mechanisms that are thought to be functioning abnormally in people with ADHD.

GENETICS

As thirteen-year-old David stood before his classmates delivering a speech, his facial gestures and mannerisms clearly identified him as his father's son. Their resemblance was unmistakable. "And that's not all that's the same," commented his father, noting that David shared the same behavioral and learning problems that he had experienced some thirty years earlier. David was diagnosed as having both an attention deficit disorder and a learning disability at age six, and like many children with such problems, David came by it genetically. Or as he himself put it, "My dad gave me a few bad genes."

The resemblances between children's behavior and that of their parents have been acknowledged by families for generations. "He's just like his father was" can be heard in living rooms throughout the world, as families search for an explanation of unruly behavior. But what grandmothers didn't know, and what is only now becoming accepted as scientific fact, is that similar behavioral characteristics from one generation to the next result from more than similar upbringing. Behavior and personality are, in large part, actually written into a person's genetic blueprint. Just as David inherited his eye color and bone structure from his father, so he inherited the temperamental characteristics that led to his diagnosis of ADHD.

Note that we do not say that David "got ADHD" from his father. One doesn't simply *get* ADHD. Environmental, psychological, and social factors play important roles in determining whether a child's behavioral and/or learning problems are sufficiently troublesome to warrant a diagnosis. Furthermore, the manner in which ADHD and its associated temperamental characteristics are inherited remains unclear.

But as scientists study the inheritance patterns of ADHD by looking at the parents and siblings of ADHD children and by studying twins and adoptees, they have suggested—but not proved—a genetic basis of ADHD.

One study, for example, compared the parents and siblings of ADD children with the parents and siblings of normal children. Among the relatives of the normal children, the incidence of ADD approximated the known incidence of ADD in the general population—about 6 percent. But among the relatives of the ADD children, the incidence was over 70 percent.[3] Although we cannot rule out the effects that being raised by a parent with ADHD has on a child, this study suggests a strong familial pattern of attention deficit disorders.

In studies of hyperactivity and inattentiveness in twins, several investigators have noted that identical twins are much more alike than are fraternal twins and that these similarities cannot simply be explained by the popular tendency to assume that identical twins look, think, and act alike. Moreover, in studies of adopted-away children with attention deficit disorders, the biological parents were more likely than the adoptive parents to exhibit symptoms of attention deficit disorders or related psychiatric conditions. These three studies support the theory that a child may be born with the tendency to develop ADHD and that he inherits that tendency from his parents.

Geneticists have been able to deduce the patterns of inheritance of some diseases by tracking the disease through several generations, but the pattern of ADHD inheritance is less clear. Although fathers and sons exhibit symptoms more frequently than do mothers and daughters, this pattern probably relates more to the higher incidence of the disorder in males than to the form of inheritance. It may be that the gene or genes responsible for ADHD are inherited by both boys and girls but that the symptoms are more often expressed in boys than in girls. What influences symptom expression has yet to be determined, but we do know that each child has a unique constellation of symptoms, strengths, and difficulties that appear to be strongly influenced by psychosocial factors not under genetic control. This means that while you, as a parent, cannot change your child's genetic tendency toward ADHD, you may be able to manipulate other factors that can influence the expression of symptoms.

BIOLOGY

Genetics may help explain why certain children are inattentive, impulsive, and hyperactive, but it does nothing to describe what actually goes wrong within the brain. Studies of how the brain controls behavior and attention have been conducted for many years, but little is actually known. Even though chemical, anatomical, and developmental defects have all been implicated in the pathogenesis of ADHD, no one has conclusively demonstrated any basic, primary deficit. It may be that many neurological factors interact or that any one of several different neurological defects can cause ADHD.

One popular theory holds that ADHD results from a delay in the maturation of the systems within the brain that control attention. Like other skills that develop over time as a child grows, attentional processes mature gradually as a child moves from exploring his environment to more goal-directed activities. A young child cannot fix his concentration on any one activity for a prolonged period of time because he is still in the exploring stage. As he grows older his attention span should improve. But if his attentional processes mature more slowly than usual, he might attend less well than would be expected of a child his age. This developmental-lag theory might explain why some of the symptoms of ADHD, especially hyperactivity, diminish with time. If delayed maturation is indeed found to be a cause of ADHD, it may be that for people who continue to have ADHD as adults, development never catches up but remains impaired throughout their lifespan.

But this theory still does not explain what processes in the brain control attention. In order to understand the neurophysiology of attention, scientists have focused on neurotransmitters—chemicals in the brain that allow nerves to communicate with one another. An imbalance of two of the key neurotransmitters, dopamine and norepinephrine, has been suggested as responsible for ADHD as well as for related conditions such as learning disabilities and tic disorders. Dopamine levels appear to influence motor control and the restraint of impulses, while norepinephrine levels more strongly influence emotionality. The relative balance of the two could explain the different patterns of ADHD—that is, why some children are more impulsive and hyperactive while others are more emotionally reactive.

Drugs that are used to treat hyperactivity are known to act at the level of neurotransmitters, lending support to the idea that imbalances in neurotransmitter levels are at the root of ADHD. But Ritalin (methylphenidate) affects so many different aspects of brain function and neurotransmission that it has been difficult to determine from its use which aspects are most critical to the development of ADHD. Other drugs with more specific modes of action have not been shown to be as effective for as many people as has Ritalin. This suggests that different aspects of neurotransmission may be affected in different people.

Very recent evidence has shown that hyperactivity is associated with decreased sugar metabolism in areas of the brain that are known to regulate attention and motor activity.[4] This research, which used a sophisticated brain imaging device known as a PET scanner (PET stands for "positron-emission tomography") has provided the first clear evidence of a neurobiological difference between hyperactive and normal people, and it should open the doors to a clearer understanding of the causes of ADHD.

Scientists in this recent study as well as in earlier studies have tried to determine whether a specific area of the brain is affected in people with ADHD. The frontal lobe appears to be the most likely candidate because it is that part of the brain that controls attention and inhibits overreactivity. Moreover, people who have suffered known damage in that part of the brain often display signs of hyperactivity, inattentiveness, and impulsivity. More precise localization has been attempted, but so far it has not yielded conclusive results.

In sum, the neurological basis of ADHD is still a mystery, despite many efforts to identify a basic dysfunction. The reasons for this persistent lack of clarity are many. For one, the tools available to scientists are far too crude to allow a detailed study of the brain in people who are basically normal. For another, neurotransmitters act at minuscule concentrations, making their levels nearly impossible to measure. Finally, the neurological basis of ADHD may be completely different in different people. In other psychiatric illnesses, such as bipolar disease (manic-depressive illness), a cause was implicated only after an effective drug treatment was discovered. But as we have seen, stimulants work so nonspecifically that they have yielded few clues about the basis of ADHD.

OTHER POSSIBLE CAUSES

While most cases of ADHD can probably be attributed to inborn temperamental characteristics and thus to genetics, there are some other causes of attentional problems and hyperactivity. You will want to determine whether your child's difficulties can be attributed to any of these other factors, since it will influence the course of treatment you select for your child.

BRAIN DAMAGE As we have seen in chapter 2, brain damage is known to lead to symptoms of hyperactivity, inattentiveness, and impulsivity. In fact, it was the association of these symptoms with brain injury and brain infection that led to the disorder being called "minimal brain damage" for a number of years. As a result of this association, inattention and hyperactivity were thought to be signs that brain damage had occurred, and attempts were made to identify the possible causes of brain damage. It is *not* clear at this time what proportion of children with ADHD have sustained brain damage.

Minor or major brain damage can result from a variety of conditions that occur before, during, or after birth. Some people feel that ADHD is at the mild end of a continuum of brain-injury disorders that range up to severe developmental disorders like cerebral palsy. In many cases of brain damage, the cause is never truly known, and in the case of ADHD, the presence or absence of brain damage may never be confirmed. Nevertheless, the following are known as possible causes of brain damage and presumably could cause some minor abnormalities even if obvious brain damage cannot be confirmed.

Some genetic disorders that affect neurological development may result in hyperactivity and inattentiveness. This category includes a chromosomal disorder called Fragile X syndrome, which is thought to be responsible for many cases of mental retardation. On occasion, children with Fragile X syndrome may be only mildly affected, in which case ADHD symptoms may predominate.

In a developing baby, brain damage may occur as a result of an infection in the mother or from drugs taken by the mother. This latter category includes prescription drugs as well as drugs of abuse such as alcohol and cocaine. Babies born with fetal alcohol syndrome, a multiply-handicapping condition that may occur when a mother drinks during pregnancy, are known to suffer from severe behavioral problems including hyperactivity. Possibly, alcohol that an expectant mother consumes at lower concentrations might produce similar, although perhaps less severe, behavioral difficulties in the child. At birth, any condition that results in oxygen deprivation can lead to brain damage.

During childhood, brain damage and/or symptoms of ADHD can result from head injury or infection. In addition, metabolic disorders such as hyperammonemia (in which the lack of a necessary enzyme leads to the buildup of ammonia) or hyperthyroidism (in which the thyroid gland overproduces its hormone), or exposure to environmental toxins may lead to minor or major brain abnormalities. Several studies have linked lead, a strong neurotoxin, with behavioral problems including hyperactivity. Lead can be found in the peeling and chipping paint of older homes that were painted with lead-based paints, as well as in the solder used in years past to weld water pipes. Lead-containing gasolines have contributed to high levels of airborne lead in some polluted areas. Because lead is so widespread in our environment, it may be a significant cause of behavioral problems among children.

DIET The role of diet in ADHD etiology remains controversial, despite extensive research and experience. In 1974, the pediatrician Benjamin Feingold published the book *Why Your Child Is Hyperactive,* which claimed that certain food additives, dyes, and artificial flavors cause hyperactivity. Feingold proposed that hyperactive children be put on a diet free of these substances. Though the diet is difficult to maintain, it appeared to alleviate behavioral problems in many children. But controlled studies intended to prove Feingold's hypothesis have yielded mixed results, and most scientists believe the Feingold diet is ineffective.

Still, some evidence does exist that under certain conditions, food can influence behavior. On the one hand, good nutrition can protect a growing child from diseases that may cause symptoms of ADHD. It may also protect a child from the effects of certain toxins in the environment; for example, the mineral zinc, which is found in whole wheat and other foods, is believed to protect against the harmful effects of the heavy metal cadmium. On the other hand, nutritional deficiencies can lead to behavioral as well as physical problems. For example, an iron deficiency can lead to inattention, restlessness, and aggression.

But whether certain foods *cause* hyperactivity or inattention is still open to question. Refined sugar has often been suggested as a cause of hyperactivity in children. While controlled studies have failed to prove a direct sugar connection, the number of anecdotes from parents that suggest it are too numerous to discount. It may be that high-sugar foods in combination with other dietary factors or given in certain situations, such as when the child is already highly stressed, may increase a child's behavioral problems to some degree or push him to the threshold over which his behavior becomes troublesome.

Caffeine—found in some cola beverages, coffee, chocolate, and tea—has also been suggested as a cause of overactivity. Although caffeine is a stimulant, there is no evidence to support this idea. In fact, caffeine is often suggested as a possible *treatment*. Like the other stimulants used to treat ADHD, caffeine has been shown to increase vigilance and attentiveness in both children and adults. It appears to be less effective than other stimulant medications, however, and in the doses required to produce a beneficial effect, it is associated with significant side effects.

In recent years, the artificial sweetener aspartame has come under increasing scrutiny as a possible cause of hyperactivity or inattentiveness. From a theoretical standpoint, aspartame does appear a likely candidate. It is made up of two amino acids, phenylalanine and aspartic acid, that play important roles in the brain's synthesis of neurotransmitters. And while aspartame was extensively studied for physical and cancer-causing effects before it was introduced on the market in 1974, its effects on behavior have not been well studied. In his 1989 book *Feeding the Brain: How Foods Affect Children,* C. Keith Conners describes children who appear to suffer extreme reactions to aspartame, including behavioral problems, seizures, and headaches.[5] But in a few controlled studies, no consistent problems were observed. Conners suggests that some people may be especially sensitive to aspartame but that, in general, any aspartame effect is probably subtle and minimal.

Despite the lack of scientific evidence that any dietary component is a major cause of ADHD, many people continue to believe that manipulation of children's diet can influence their behavior. It may be that adherence to a very controlled diet, like the Feingold diet, yields a benefit because the extra attention that the child receives helps him to control his inborn tendency toward inattentiveness and overactivity. In addition, a dietary explanation allows parents to view the child as "ill" rather than "bad," thus reducing some of the social and emotional stress on the child.

MEDICATIONS Some medications given to treat other health problems can elicit overactive and inattentive behavior. These drugs include theophylline, given to treat asthma; cold or allergy preparations that contain ephedrine, pseudoephedrine, or ethanolamine; and anticonvulsants. Theophylline and the cold medications can act as stimulants, while anticonvulsants tend to be sedating and thus can decrease attentiveness.

PSYCHOSOCIAL CAUSES OF ADHD-LIKE BEHAVIORS In some cases, inattentiveness, distractibility, and hyperactivity occur in reaction to a specific situation rather than to an inborn tendency toward these problems. For example, a child in an extremely chaotic or disrupted home environment, such as an alcoholic or abusive home, or a child who has undergone a significant change in his life (such as a divorce or move), may act up primarily as a means of attracting attention and expressing frustration. In such cases, the symptoms of ADHD may be masking an anxiety disorder. Such was the case with six-year-old Jeffrey, who had started kindergarten at a new school. Although he was a bright boy, his teachers noted that he had trouble getting along with the other children, became easily frustrated, and was easily provoked, jittery, and inattentive. The school psychologist suspected that Jeffrey had ADHD and suggested that his parents see a doctor in order to try medication. But Jeffrey's pediatrician felt uncomfortable with this diagnosis and called the ADHD Clinic at The Children's Hospital of Philadelphia for a consultation. The psychologist who met Jeffrey there noted that he had no prior history of distractibility or inattention. He suggested that Jeffrey's inattentive behavior might be the result of frustration or anxiety arising from difficulty adjusting to the new school. The psychologist suggested trying some behavior-management approaches, including carefully structuring Jeffrey's environment and monitoring his behavior. Within several weeks, Jeffrey's troublesome behavior subsided, and he became more relaxed and happy at school.

Another possible psychosocial cause of behavioral problems is a chaotic or poorly structured environment, which may bring out the symptoms in a child who already tends toward ADHD. Such situations that can give rise to problems may occur at home, at school, or elsewhere in the child's environment, such as on the playground. In school, a highly structured and rigid classroom may frustrate a child with mild attentional difficulties to the point that he acts in an uncontrollable fashion. An extremely unstructured environment may allow that same child to become so distracted and overactive that he again loses control. Yet he may function quite well in a less rigid environment, where he is allowed to be somewhat active but where limits are clearly defined and adhered to.

Some studies have suggested that children's interaction with their mothers may cause behavioral problems. In these studies, mothers of children with attention deficits were observed to be more critical and disapproving, less affectionate, and to punish more severely than other mothers. In addition, the mothers reported having low confidence in their parenting skills, high levels of stress, and feelings of isolation and depression. Unfortunately, in these studies cause and effect are difficult to separate. It may be that such mothers' parenting styles first developed as a reaction to the child's unruly behavior, but that over time, their rigidity and lack of affection began to contribute to the child's difficulties.

Finally, it is important to note that different parenting styles between mother and father can contribute to a child's behavioral difficulties. For example, when one parent is rigid and another permissive, the child may be in a constant state of confusion about the limits to which he must adhere. This confusion can lead to disruptive behavior.

The cause of most children's attentional difficulties is never known with certainty. Indeed, many factors may coexist. Considering the many causes of ADHD may help point you toward the most effective treatments. In part II of this book, we look at the many different types of treatment that are available and discuss the value of taking a multifaceted approach to management.

PART II
Managing ADHD

CHAPTER 4

Finding Help

So you think your child may have attention deficits or hyper-activity. Maybe a teacher has suggested that you get him tested; maybe you just suspect it from your own observations. Whatever the reason for your suspicions, you need help. But where do you turn? In this chapter we will discuss strategies you might use to try to find the right care-provider. But before you look, you should think about what you expect from treatment and what approach will be most appropriate for your child.

EXPECTATIONS AND GOALS OF TREATMENT

Treating ADHD will not make it go away. The characteristics that lead most children to be diagnosed as having ADHD are inborn behavioral and temperamental characteristics that are part of who they are. These characteristics will stay with them throughout their lives, even as the problems fluctuate over the years. Treatment can help improve a child's chances for avoiding some of the long-term problems that can result from having ADHD. You will likely need long-term help in man-aging your child, either through ongoing therapy or periodic consultation.

Treating ADHD does not mean simply correcting a problem that the child has. After all, it is not only the symptoms themselves that are problematic, but how those symptoms create problems in the context of the child's environment. Therefore, the goal of treatment is to help the child fit into his environment more comfortably and to reduce the likelihood that he will develop secondary symptoms of depression, anxiety, and poor self-esteem. Managing the child with ADHD involves a combination of adjusting or modifying his behaviors and manipulating his environment in order to achieve this better fit. The treatment process should also give parents tools that can help them deal more effectively with the child's difficulties.

In other words, it is not only the child who has to change. Family members and teachers must also be willing to look at how their actions may influence the child's difficulties. For instance, at school the child may have difficulty paying attention to instructions and therefore may miss assignments and fall behind. Treatment may address the child's basic inattentiveness, but in addition, it may involve helping teachers find better ways of encouraging, rather than discouraging, compliance. At home, the goal of treatment may be to change the climate of the family from one of constant frustration and anger to one of more reason, hope, and tolerance. This involves adjusting parental expectations to a level that the child can reach and learning how to deal with conflict more constructively.

There is no single correct way of treating all children with ADHD. Children with ADHD are more different than they are alike. While the name *ADHD* lumps them together, each child has different strengths and weaknesses that must be considered when designing a program that will help that child reach his full potential. Treatment also has to be tailored to the family's resources. In most cases, treatment must address multiple issues in the child's life.

THE VALUE OF MULTIMODAL THERAPY

Because ADHD usually affects multiple areas of a child's life, treatment should also be multifaceted. Treatment for ADHD may involve medication, for example, but medication usually addresses only some of the child's difficulties. It may help control the child's basic overactivity and inattentiveness, but it does not supply him with the behavioral, social, and educational skills he needs to function better in society. These skills can best be addressed through the coordinated efforts of doctors, teachers, mental health professionals, and parents. The Children's Hospital of Philadelphia and its affiliates have designed such a program; together with the child and his parents, the pediatricians, psychologists, psychiatrists, and social workers at the Hospital make up the kind of "treatment team" that can work together to maximize a child's chance of success.

This prescription for a multimodal approach to treatment is based not only on common sense and experience but on research as well. In several studies, medication alone has been shown to have only modest long-term beneficial effects on overactivity and impulsivity and very little impact on the social and academic aspects of children's lives. Only a few studies have compared how different treatment approaches affect long-term outcome, but those studies have been revealing. James Satterfield, for one, followed a group of hyperactive and aggressive boys for many years.[6] He divided the boys into two treatment groups: those who received drugs only, and those who received multimodal treatment. For the latter group, multimodal treatment programs were individually devised for each boy after a thorough evaluation of his areas of need. The programs consisted of medication, individual or group therapy, educational therapy, and/or family therapy. Satterfield followed the boys for approximately nine years and evaluated their arrest records as a measure of delinquency. He showed that the group of boys who had received only drug treatment were arrested and institutionalized for felony offenses such as robbery, burglary, theft, and assault more frequently than were the boys who had received multimodal treatment. Further, he showed that boys who received more than two years of multimodal treatment had an even better outcome than did the boys who stopped treatment before two years.

While Satterfield's study focused on a certain subgroup of ADHD boys—that is, those who were also aggressive and/or conduct-disordered—the fact that he was able to show a benefit from multimodal treatment may mean that it can provide other children with ADHD with similar benefits. Other long-term studies have also indicated that children who receive multimodal treatment have a better long-term outcome than do children who are treated with medication alone.

Multimodal treatment has other potential advantages: It may allow a child to rely less heavily on medication as a way of controlling his behavior. It can reinforce a feeling of mastery in a child. He may be able to appreciate that he has some control over his difficulties, that he is not "dependent" on the medication to keep him in check.

In the introduction to this book, you met ten-year-old Alex who, in fourth grade, experienced mounting difficulties in school. By the time Alex came to the ADHD Clinic for evaluation and treatment, his parents felt hopeless. His teachers had tried some behavior-modification approaches to improve his attentiveness but had given up because these approaches hadn't worked. Alex was doing increasingly poorly academically and was frequently unhappy and irritable. Yet Alex's mother didn't want him medicated. She worried about the side effects and that he would become dependent on the medication.

The psychologist observed Alex in school, spoke with his teachers, and enlisted their support in trying another behavioral-treatment program. Alex and his parents met with the psychologist several times, worked out the bugs in the system, and implemented it. Alex began earning rewards at home for much improved behavior at school, and he seemed to feel much better about himself. But he continued to have trouble focusing on his work at school, and there was still room for improvement in his behavior. Alex and his parents then met with a pediatrician, who upon examining him concluded that he had no unusual medical reason for his inattentiveness and had nothing that would preclude the use of medicine. After the pediatrician had discussed the pros and cons of medicating Alex, his parents decided to go ahead with a carefully controlled medication trial.

Three dosage levels were tried. Alex performed as well on the low dose as he did on the moderate and relatively high doses. Therefore, he continued with a low dose until the completion of the school year, when he was even awarded "Student of the Month" in May. Alex, his parents, and his teachers were all thrilled with his progress. In addition, they felt a measure of pride because it was through their joint efforts that Alex had been able to have such a happy outcome. The behavior-treatment program had enhanced their feelings of competence; all sensed that they had played important roles in Alex's progress. And Alex's parents were relieved that he could get by on such a low dose of medicine. Though it is difficult to prove, his doctors believe that it may have been because of the early success with the behavior program that Alex was able to improve with such a small amount of medicine.

FINDING A CARE-PROVIDER

In looking for the appropriate professional to coordinate your child's care, there are several factors you will want to keep in mind. First, is the care-provider competent and experienced in treating ADHD? Second, does he offer multiple approaches to treatment, and will he oversee a multimodal approach?

Your first candidate may be your own *pediatrician* or *family doctor*. If this is your choice, ask him if he has experience with and feels comfortable in treating ADHD. He may prefer to refer you to someone more knowledgeable, or he may recommend an outside consultation. Some pediatricians, especially those who specialize in developmental pediatrics, are very knowledgeable about ADHD and have developed their own systems for treating it. Family practitioners may also have the advantage of knowing your child over a long period of time. But though developmental pediatricians can often diagnose ADHD and prescribe medicine, they may not have the capacity to do the psychological, behavioral, educational, and social assessments and interventions that may be necessary. In addition, some pediatricians may be reluctant to medicate your child and may want additional input from a psychologist who can make medication recommendations or a psychiatrist who can prescribe medicine.

Some pediatricians will refer patients with suspected ADHD to a *child neurologist.* While child neurologists are generally very familiar with ADHD and can rule out other possible medical problems and prescribe medicine, they are not likely to use behavioral and educational strategies in treatment. Neurologists are particularly useful whenever there is an indication that a child's difficulties are more neurologically based—for instance, if the child has symptoms that suggest a seizure disorder or some sort of brain damage, or if the child has a complicating neurological problem such as Tourette syndrome.

Child psychiatrists have the medical degree that allows them to prescribe medicine. They have the orientation toward psychological management, and the experience of treating large numbers of ADHD children. But child psychiatrists usually are not pediatricians, and they will not give you the overall medical assessment that may be required. Nevertheless, psychiatrists are usually quick to spot physical problems that may need further evaluation. They are also useful if the child has serious psychiatric problems in addition to inattentiveness and hyperactivity, such as severe depression or anxiety. In addition, a child psychiatrist may be appropriate if the family is under severe stress as a result of, or in addition to, having problems with the child's ADHD.

Child psychologists are often the professionals most familiar with ADHD, and they may be the most comfortable with behavioral, educational, and social approaches to treatment. But psychologists cannot prescribe medicine and cannot provide the medical assessment that pediatricians can provide.

If you don't have a pediatrician who feels comfortable treating ADHD, there are several ways that you can locate the right person. One good source of information is a parent-support group in your area or other organizations that advocate for children with ADHD (see chapter 13). Your school psychologist or guidance counselor may be able to recommend someone. If you know of other parents who have children with ADHD, ask them for suggestions as well.

Many large medical centers have comprehensive ADHD programs like the one operated jointly by The Children's Hospital of Philadelphia, the Philadelphia Child Guidance Clinic, and the Children's Seashore House in Philadelphia. If you live near one of these medical centers, you may want to investigate to see if it offers services that would be appropriate for your child. Even if you decide that you don't want to take your child to that medical center, someone there may be able to recommend a good care-provider in your area.

You may be lucky enough to find a professional who recognizes the value of multimodal intervention and will coordinate it for you. For example, some pediatricians have established working relationships with psychologists who specialize in the treatment of children with ADHD. Or you may come across a school counselor who has worked effectively with a certain pediatrician or child psychologist. If you don't find such a person, you may be able to initiate a multimodal treatment program yourself. For instance, you might get a psychological evaluation for your child, then ask the psychologist to write a letter to your pediatrician outlining his findings and suggesting a treatment course. The psychologist might recommend a medication trial, outline the steps that would be required, and suggest a way to monitor the effectiveness of the medication. He might also write a letter to your child's teacher or guidance counselor with suggestions for in-school behavior strategies.

This strategy of using a psychologist as a consultant can also be valuable if you cannot find the right care-provider in your area and don't want to travel the distance required to visit a comprehensive care center.

Finding the professionals who can or will use multimodal strategies in treating your child may be difficult. You may have to follow a multimodal strategy yourself in order to ensure that your child's pediatrician, school counselors, teachers, and psychologist, if necessary, are working toward the same goal and complementing one another's efforts. But you do not want to get into the position of carrying messages from one professional to the other. Ask them to contact and consult with one another. Your role should be to make sure your child is getting coordinated and comprehensive care—you should not have to design his treatment program yourself.

CHAPTER 5

Diagnosing ADHD

Neil had always been considered "wild" and "hyper" by his preschool teachers, but otherwise he had seemed happy and well adjusted—just a bit "immature." At age four, however, his teachers began to wonder if Neil was more than extremely energetic. They suggested to his parents that he might have an attention deficit disorder. So began the long journey through the diagnostic maze that confronts parents whose children are thought to have ADHD or related problems. For several months, Neil and his parents went from one specialist to the next and endured many hours of testing, only to find that none of the tests yielded a clear answer. Although Neil was given a diagnosis of ADHD so that his parents could get reimbursed from the insurance company, the testing had not provided a clear explanation of Neil's difficulties. What it had shown was that he had no clear neurological problem, that he had normal intelligence but academic skills that were below what were expected of a child his age, and that he appeared to have trouble paying attention in class.

Neil's story illustrates several problems associated with the diagnosis of ADHD. For starters, ADHD is difficult to diagnose in a child as young as four; overactivity, inattention, and impulsivity are all fairly "normal" characteristics of four-year-olds. But even for older children, the diagnosis of ADHD is problematic. No test exists that says "absolutely, this child does (or does not) have ADHD." Further, while children with ADHD share some similarities, they can also be as different as snowflakes. Neil's diagnostic adventure probably yielded enough information from which his doctors could determine how to proceed. But it didn't produce what his parents had been expecting: a definitive answer about his difficulties and a clear-cut prescription for treatment.

Although we have emphasized that little is gained by focusing on the question of whether a child has ADHD in earlier chapters of this book, the diagnostic process is important to undergo. It orients the child, his parents, and his care-providers to the general nature of his difficulties. It tells parents that their child has a constellation of behaviors about which a fair amount is known; that there are steps they can take to increase their understanding of their child's difficulties; and that they can learn to manage him more effectively. Further, the diagnosis can help direct parents to a body of literature about the disorder and to other sources of support.

The diagnostic process also serves to rule out medical or psychiatric problems that might otherwise go undetected for some time. For example, children with brain tumors or seizure disorders may show symptoms of inattentiveness and hyperactivity long before any more serious complications appear. Fortunately, these conditions occur very rarely. Somewhat more common, though still rare, is the child who suffers from an undetected hearing or visual impairment. Again, this child may appear to be inattentive, or he may act up behaviorally as a means of showing his frustration. The diagnostic process can alert parents to his real problem. The process may also uncover more serious emotional or behavioral difficulties—for instance a depressed or anxious child, or one who has learning difficulties that are interfering with his school performance.

Diagnosis can provide information about a child's strengths and weaknesses. It can help identify which situations are particularly problematic for him, and which situa-

tions are easier. It may identify his part
strengths and weaknesses that may affect hi
ferent situations.

Finally, the diagnostic process can help determine
types of intervention will be most appropriate for the child.
For one child, medication might be ruled out as an option
because of a complicating medical factor. For another child,
the school situation may be insufficiently flexible to accommodate certain in-school behavioral approaches. Still another
child might need academic tutoring or remedial help to help
him overcome a learning disability.

In other words, diagnosing ADHD involves not only testing the child for certain characteristics, but also evaluating
aspects of his social, educational, and family environment and
finding effective interventions for his difficulties.

THE STEPS IN DIAGNOSIS

Every health care professional who treats children with
ADHD has a different method for evaluating children. The
Children's Hospital of Philadelphia, Philadelphia Child
Guidance Clinic and Children's Seashore House follow a
"case management" model, in which one member of the
team—usually a pediatrician, psychologist, or social worker—
assesses and evaluates the child's difficulties and then, in consultation with the rest of the team, determines what, if any,
further evaluations are needed. The case manager then coor-
dinates the various psychological, educational, and medical
assessments and treatment interventions.

The process often starts with an initial consultation between the case manager, the parents, and the child. Usually,
parents and teachers are asked to complete questionnaires
that assess the scope of the child's problems. Depending on
what appears necessary, the child may then undergo other
evaluations. If the troublesome behaviors appear to be linked
to a medical problem, such as a seizure disorder or allergies,
or if medication is indicated, a full medical evaluation is per-

ormed. Many children also need a full psychological evaluation. If psychological testing has already been performed, the treatment team reviews the test results in order to determine if additional testing is warranted. A psychiatric evaluation or a more in-depth neurological exam may be ordered in some cases. Below, we describe each of these steps in some detail. But you should be aware that your child may not need each evaluation. Moreover, other health practitioners may follow a different model. If your family physician is supervising your child's care, he may feel that he already has enough information about your child and does not need any further evaluations.

THE CONSULTATION: IDENTIFYING THE PROBLEM

The purpose of the initial consultation is to determine what has led the parents to seek treatment, how they view the child's problems, and what they have already done to deal with the difficulties. In addition, the case manager tries to develop a picture of the family unit, including background information about the family, information about the child's brothers and sisters, and how the child's difficulties affect the entire family. From the initial consultation, the case manager can determine how best to proceed and which types of diagnostic evaluations are needed.

In such a consultation, you might be asked to describe the situations that present the most difficulty for your child and what his difficulties are. For example, if his biggest problem is at school, the case manager will want to know whether your child has difficulty getting the work done, if he disrupts the class, or if he fights with other children. Do the problems occur in the classroom, on the playground, or in the cafeteria? Are there situations at school in which your child has no problems? These kinds of questions can help the case manager know if your child might need further psychoeducational testing or if behavior management might be in order.

In addition to pinpointing the areas of difficulty, the case manager will try to determine the severity of the symptoms. Rating scales, described below, also may be used to assess severity. The initial consultation will include questions about the level of stress within your family, the availability of family or community support, and the resources of your family. You may be asked about your parenting skills and disciplining techniques. All these factors play a role in determining what kinds of intervention your child may need. For example, a mildly affected child with skillful parents may need only behavioral therapy, while such a child from a stressed family may need other forms of intervention as well. Even the most highly skilled parents may be unable to deal constructively with a severely affected child and may need medication and behavior therapy for the child, as well as support for themselves, in order to manage the child successfully.

The initial consultation also presents an opportunity for parents to discuss their own desires and expectations. For example, if you are opposed to the use of medication for your child, this is the time to relay that information to the case manager. Or if you are mainly concerned with your child's performance in school but feel you can handle him at home, you should make this known. Typically, parents have multiple goals in seeking treatment. The initial consultation offers them an opportunity to establish priorities so that the most pressing problems can be dealt with first.

THE BEHAVIORAL ASSESSMENT

Because ADHD is by definition a behavioral issue, the best way to determine whether a child has ADHD-like symptoms is to study his behavior using naturalistic measures. These assessment methods evaluate the child in the context of his own environment rather than in the unnatural and unfamiliar setting of the doctor's office or clinic. Methods of behavioral assessment include questionnaires given to parents, teachers, and sometimes to the children themselves, that rate a child's behavior; and professional observation of the child in a natural setting—at school, on the playground, or at home.

RATING SCALES Rating scales are used to identify the nature and the scope of a child's difficulty both at home and at school. As discussed in chapter 2, the first rating scale commonly used to assess hyperactivity was the Conners Teacher Rating Scale (CTRS, also sometimes referred to as the Conners Teacher Questionnaire, or CTQ), which was developed in 1969. The original Conners scale listed thirty-nine behaviors that were supposed to characterize a hyperkinetic child. Over the years, the Conners scale has been revised and other rating scales have been introduced, including scales that assess the parents' perception of the child's problems.

Ideally, both the child's parents and his teachers fill out rating scales. Frequently, the parents' perceptions and the teachers' perceptions differ markedly. These differences can be easily understood if one considers the different demands placed on the child in the two environments. When only one rating scale is obtained—for example, only a parent rating scale—many of the child's difficulties can be missed. Although parents may think they know about the problems a teacher is having with their child, frequently they know only a fraction of the difficulties. Teachers are also in a better position to rate a child's behavior as it compares with that of other children his age.

Parent rating scales that are commonly used include the Conners Parent Symptom Questionnaire, the Swanson, Nolan, and Pelham (SNAP) rating scale, the Achenbach Child Behavior Checklist (CBCL), and the Home Situations Questionnaire. Teacher rating scales include the Conners Teacher Questionnaire, the Child Activity-Attention Profile (CAAP), the ADDH Comprehensive Teacher Rating Scales (ACTeRS), and the School Situations Questionnaire. These rating scales are not interchangeable, although they all assess roughly the same characteristics: inattention, impulsivity, and hyperactivity. The CBCL also assesses other characteristics such as social withdrawal, depression, anxiety, and conduct problems and thus gives a broader measure of the child's difficulties, while the CAAP and the Conners look more narrowly at the symptoms of ADHD.

Each of the scales is evaluated in a different manner. A description of how the Conners Teacher Rating Scale (CTRS) is used will illustrate in a general way how all these scales are used. The teacher's questonnaire lists twenty-eight behaviors and asks the teacher to rate a child for each of these items. Figure 1 shows a portion of the rating scale. For each item on the list, the teacher gives the child a score of 0 where the "not at all" column is checked, 1 for "just a little," 2 for "pretty much," and 3 for "very much."

Of these twenty-eight questions, ten relate specifically to hyperactivity. The evaluator totals the scores from these ten questions to obtain a subscore called the Hyperactivity Index. The lowest subscore possible is 0; the highest 30. By applying the rating scale to thousands of school-age children, researchers have determined the average score for children of each age and sex and have determined age-appropriate cutoff scores. Above this cutoff, a child would be judged hyperactive.

Other subscores can also be calculated from the rating scale information. A different group of questions relate to disruptive, uncooperative, and quarrelsome behavior. When the scores for these questions are totaled, the evaluator can develop a "conduct problems" subscore. Likewise, adding up the scores from another group of questions can yield a measure of inattention and passivity. Some of the items on the list relate to more than one behavioral problem; for instance, the symptom "Temper outbursts and unpredictable behavior" is included in both the hyperactivity and conduct problems subscores.

While these scores may give the impression of objectivity and definitiveness, they should be viewed with some skepticism. Anyone who looks at the list of behaviors can see that different people might interpret them differently. Behavior

Conners Teacher Rating Scale (fig. 1)

Teacher's Questionnaire

Name of Child _____ Grade _____

Date of Evaluation _____

Please answer all questions. Beside *each* item, indicate the degree of the problem by a check mark (✓)

	Not at all	Just a little	Pretty much	Very much
1. Restless in the "squirmy" sense.				
2. Makes inappropriate noises when he shouldn't.				
3. Demands must be met immediately.				
4. Acts "smart" (impudent or sassy).				
5. Temper outbursts and unpredictable behavior.				
6. Overly sensitive to criticism.				

that may seem excessive to one teacher or parent may seem quite acceptable to another. One teacher might think a child daydreams "very much," while another teacher would say he daydreams "just a little." Therefore, rating-scale information should not be the sole basis of a diagnosis. It can, however, alert parents and care-providers to the general nature of a child's difficulties. Further, it may be used as "baseline" information for purposes of comparison with rating-scale data obtained after the child has begun treatment.

DIRECT OBSERVATION School-based direct observation of the child in his natural environment is one of the most valuable types of behavioral assessment, but it is probably one of the least used. Because it involves having the psychologist visit the school and observe your child in class and/or on the playground, it can be quite costly. Nevertheless, it can provide extremely valuable information that will be useful if behavioral treatment is considered. The psychologist who has visited a child's school will know what he is working with— what the academic demands of the school are, how skilled the teachers are in managing the child's behavior, and other aspects of the school environment that may influence a child's ability to pay attention and/or stay out of trouble. The visit may also allow the psychologist to establish a good working relationship with the child's teachers and with other important people at the school, such as the principal or guidance counselor.

Observation methods vary among different psychologists. Some simply watch and take anecdotal notes about the child's activities and behaviors. Others use a more systematic approach, such as a tally sheet upon which they check off the incidence of specific behavioral events such as the child getting out of his seat, speaking out either appropriately or inappropriately, or focusing on something besides the teacher or the lesson.

A second type of direct-observational behavioral assessment involves setting up a simulated work or play experience for the child in the doctor's office or clinic. For instance, a psychologist might set the child up in a playroom where he can observe from behind a one-way mirror. If the parents are with the child in the playroom, the psychologist can see how well the child complies with parental commands. Or the child might be requested to complete some tasks while the psychologist observes the child's ability to stay "on task."

Simulated behavioral assessments can be logistically simpler than a school visit, but not all clinics have the facilities to do them properly. Further, a child's performance on simulated tasks may not predict his performance in the more arousing environment of the elementary classroom.

THE COMPLETE PEDIATRIC EXAM

The pediatrician will want to meet with both you and your child to gather information about your child's previous medical history and current condition. This is one of the most valuable parts of the evaluation for ADHD, particularly if your pediatrician is knowledgeable about the disorder. He will be trying to corroborate your suspicions, determine whether there are any physical or neurological components to your child's attention problems, and see if there are any reasons he should avoid medication.

Some physicians take an extremely detailed developmental history and conduct a lengthy physical exam. A new doctor would be likely to do this, as would a doctor in a tertiary-care hospital, where doctors are trained to look for unsuspected or unusual problems. Other physicians conduct less extensive exams. Your family physician, for example, may feel he already knows enough about your child's health and medical history that a lengthy exam is unnecessary.

The pediatric exam described below is very comprehensive, and you should not be alarmed if your physician does not ask all the questions or perform all of the assessments described. The evaluation your child undergoes will depend on several factors, including the nature of his difficulties, the doctor's experience with ADHD children, and the doctor's previous knowledge of your child.

RANDY

Randy came to see Dr. Marianne Mercugliano at The Children's Hospital of Philadelphia after his psychologist had presented Randy's case at the ADHD team meeting and the group had agreed that medication might be useful for the ten-year-old boy. First, Dr. Mercugliano met with Randy's mother, Ellen, to try to get a general picture of Randy's difficulties and to learn more about his medical and family history. She explained to Ellen that she wanted to rule out other medical or neurological problems that might account for Randy's learning and behavioral difficulties, and she wanted to see if there were any reasons why Randy should not take medication.

The doctor asked Ellen a number of questions about her pregnancy and Randy's birth. Ellen described the pregnancy as difficult: She was often nauseated, and the baby was very active. She took antinausea medication for a short time, but other than that she took no drugs during the pregnancy, had not drunk alcohol, and had not smoked. She had received routine prenatal care and had not experienced any illnesses or infections; nor had she needed X rays or had any accidents.

Randy had been born within a few days of his due date and weighed just under seven pounds at birth. He appeared healthy at birth, and other than some jaundice in the first week, for which he received light therapy, he had no complications. He went home with Ellen after three days in the newborn nursery.

Ellen remembered that Randy cried constantly as a baby and slept poorly. Once he began to walk, at about ten months (somewhat early), he was into everything. He could climb out of his crib at one year, and he seemed somewhat accident-prone in his early years. Although Randy had no obvious allergies, he was frequently troubled by nasal congestion and sometimes by skin rashes. He had frequent ear infections for the first three years of his life. But other than these problems, he had not experienced many health problems; he had never had seizures, vision or hearing problems, or serious accidents, and had taken no significant medications other than acetaminophen and cough/cold preparations.

Dr. Mercugliano reviewed Randy's major bodily symptoms and general health with Ellen, asking her about any possible disorders of the lungs, heart, bowels, kidneys, bones, muscles, joints, blood, or skin. She also asked a number of questions that might not be asked in a standard pediatric evaluation but that pertain specifically to ADHD. For example, she asked about his moods, sleeping and eating habits, whether he threw temper tantrums or wet his bed, and whether he had nervous habits.

Randy reached his developmental milestones, including motor and speech skills, at or before the ages expected. He is right handed and fairly coordinated; he loves sports and does well in them. The only nervous habit that Ellen could recall was that he sometimes bites his nails. Ellen described Randy as sad and grumpy in the morning, and frequently sad and negativistic at other times as well. She said that Randy's teachers claim he has trouble communicating his thoughts to his classmates. He gets along well with his siblings.

Next, Dr. Mercugliano asked about Ellen's and her husband Richard's families. Ellen said she had a brother who, as a child, had gotten into trouble in school and had taken something the family called "nerve medicine." A niece and nephew of Ellen had also been diagnosed as "hyperactive." Richard's family also was sprinkled with stories of behavioral and learning problems. Richard himself had nearly gotten suspended from school in the eighth grade and had had difficulty getting through college. Neither Ellen's nor Richard's family had any history of other psychiatric disorders or substance abuse.

When Randy came into Dr. Mercugliano's office, she first asked him if he knew why he was there. Randy replied sorrowfully that he was having trouble concentrating in school. "I get in trouble more than most kids, mostly for talking and forgetting my homework," he said.

The doctor told him, "Lots of people have problems paying attention and concentrating. You're not bad or stupid. It's like your brain is doing a lot of things at once, and this sometimes makes it hard to get along with people or to do well in school." She asked him what changes he would like to see; he said he only wanted nice teachers. The physical exam that Dr. Mercugliano performed was much like any pediatric exam. She assessed Randy's overall health by weighing and measuring him and checking his ears, eyes, throat, heart, lungs, and lymph glands. She assessed his vision and hearing and watched him walk across the room to see that he moved normally. She saw that Randy was a normal-looking child, slightly small for his age but with no unusual physical features that suggested congenital abnormalities, and no signs of thyroid dysfunction or physical or sexual abuse.

During a routine neurological exam, she tested his reflexes, balance, coordination, and strength; all were normal. (Finding abnormalities in any of these neurological signs would not have been diagnostic of ADHD, but they occasionally alert a doctor to other disorders.) She saw no evidence of "neurological soft signs," such as involuntary movements or lack of coordination. These are called "soft signs" because they do not indicate a specific neurological pathology but may be signs of neurological immaturity or disorganization.

In addition to the obvious search for an illness or other significant medical problem, none of which was found, Randy's physical exam served another valuable purpose. It allowed the doctor to interact with Randy and to observe his behavior firsthand. She noted that he was a generally cooperative, pleasant child with average communication skills. He seemed sad but showed no evidence of overactivity. She knew, however, that children often act completely different in a doctor's office from the way they act in more familiar environments. Even children with significant attention deficits often appear extremely attentive when placed in an unfamiliar environment, or when faced with a man or woman wearing a white coat and possessing needles and other unfamiliar and scary tools. A doctor *cannot* make a reliable diagnosis of ADHD based solely on the child's behavior in the doctor's office.

Randy's physical exam showed him to be a healthy child, with no evidence of any medical or neurological condition that would lead to inattentiveness or behavioral problems and with no contraindications to medication. For some children, however, the medical evaluation indicates a need for more specialized testing. For instance, if a child has allergies, an exam by an allergist may be requested. Sometimes untreated allergies are so troublesome that they contribute to behavioral difficulties. If the pediatrician detects any suspicious findings that suggest an active neurological problem, she may refer the child to a neurologist for further examination and possible tests. Tests such as the electroencephalogram (EEG, or brain wave test), CT imaging (computed tomography, an X-ray-based brain-imaging study), or MRI (magnetic resonance imaging, a brain-imaging technique that does not use X rays) may be indicated if your child's history suggests the possibility of seizures or a brain tumor, or if your child has symptoms of a degenerative disease of the nervous system, or some other neurological disease.

COGNITIVE TESTING

Many children who have behavioral problems also have learning difficulties (see chapter 1). If this is the case with your child, the psychologist will probably want to give him a number of tests that measure different aspects of learning. The purpose of these tests is to determine whether your child has a specific learning disability or whether his learning difficulties relate more to problems with inattention, impulsivity, and/or hyperactivity. These tests can also reveal his particular learning style, which may help teachers, psychologists, and parents develop an appropriate educational program.

INTELLIGENCE AND ACHIEVEMENT TESTS An intelligence test is usually given first. The most commonly used intelligence tests are the Wechsler Intelligence Scale for Children–Revised (WISC-R) and the Stanford-Binet Intelligence Scale. Children under six years old may be given the Wechsler Preschool and Primary Scale of Intelligence–Revised (WPP-SI-R).

If your child is given one of these tests, the results will be reported back as IQ (Intelligence Quotient) scores. The scores from the Wechsler tests are broken down into a verbal score, a performance (nonverbal) score, and a full-scale or overall score. The verbal score represents your child's performance on subtests such as Vocabulary, Comprehension, and Similarities, while the performance score represents his spatial organization abilities as measured by subtests such as Picture Completion, Block Design, and Object Assembly. The scores reflect how your child's performance on the test compares with what is expected of an average child his age. Thus, a score of 100 signifies an average IQ; scores below 100 are termed below average, and scores above 100, above average. A score below 70 indicates mental retardation.

Your child's scores may also be analyzed to determine a "freedom from distractibility" score, which some people consider to be a reliable measure of inattention. But the validity of this measurement is questioned by many experts, who feel that it really reflects a child's ability to process symbolic information and may only indirectly relate to attention span.

Usually the verbal and performance scores are close together. Differences of more than 12 points may reflect a particular learning style. For instance, a child who processes verbal information better than he does visual information may score significantly higher on the verbal than on the performance parts of the test. But that does not mean that he has a learning disability. Learning disabilities are suggested when a child's ability or intelligence varies significantly from his performance, as assessed by achievement tests and actual school achievement.

Thus, the next tests that are usually given are achievement tests. Commonly used achievement tests are the Wide Range Achievement Test-Revised (WRAT-R), the Woodcock-Johnson Psycho-Educational Battery-Revised, and the Peabody Individual Achievement Tests (PIAT). These tests measure a child's academic skills in several areas, including reading, math, and written language. If these tests indicate that your child is achieving below his intellectual ability, further testing may be indicated to determine the nature of his learning difficulty.

MEASURES OF ATTENTION AND IMPULSIVITY In children with ADHD, learning difficulties may result not from specific learning disabilities but from other problems they have in paying attention, restraining their own tendency to respond impulsively, organizing their thoughts, planning strategies, and solving problems. Sometimes specific tests are used to evaluate the relative importance of these different aspects of functioning. These tests can help orient educational intervention to the child's specific areas of weakness even though they are not truly diagnostic for ADHD.

For example, one common test called the Matching Familiar Figures Test (MFFT) assesses a child's impulsivity. For this test, your child is presented with a card with a picture on it. He is then asked to find the correct match from among six other cards with similar pictures. In order to do well on this test, the child must inspect the pictures carefully and be able to inhibit his initial impulse to respond. Thus, the test measures not only impulsivity but the child's visual search skills.

Other tests assess different aspects of how children process information. Tests of attention and vigilance include the Continuous Performance Task (CPT) and various reaction-time tests. The CPT presents a child with a series of letters and asks him to respond to a certain target sequence—for instance, a white letter S followed by a blue letter T. This type of test is sometimes administered via computer. To perform well on the test, the child must be able to sustain his attention and control impulsive responding. Reaction-time tests assess a child's ability to react to visual stimuli after a warning signal or a suitable preparatory interval and sometimes in the presence of distractors, such as a noise. Again, the child must be able to sustain attention, screen out distractors, and limit impulsive responding.

The Selective Reminding Test measures two aspects of new learning and memory. This test consists of several rounds. In the first round, a child is given a list of twelve words and is asked to remember as many of them as she can. On the next round, the evaluator tells her which ones she missed and asks her to remember the entire list again. This goes on for eight rounds. The results of the test are evaluated in terms of how well the child has stored and retrieved the information. Some children with ADHD do well on the memory aspects of the test but poorly on the retrieval-of-information aspects. This difficulty may be related to an inability to sustain attention or to poor use of strategy. In either case, it can translate into a difficulty in completing tests and assignments.

Another test that assesses a child's ability to learn new information and sustain attention is the Paired Associate Learning Test. This test involves repeated trials of a certain memory task. For example, the child might be given a stack of ten animal pictures, which he is to place into four "zoos." On the first trial, the evaluator shows the child which animals go into which zoos. On subsequent trials, the child must try to recreate the same matches.

None of these tests is specific for ADHD, although children with ADHD tend to do more poorly than others. The test results can point to reasons for a child's learning difficulties and can suggest compensatory strategies. For instance, if your child does poorly on the Selective Reminding Test, you might conclude that the child has difficulty learning new information, particularly if that information is presented orally. Your understanding of this aspect of the child's learning style might lead you to better strategies that you or your child's teacher can use to get him to pay attention, hear directions, consistently retrieve information, stay with a task, and work through problems. These tests are often repeated and the results compared to assess the effects of medication.

THE PSYCHIATRIC EVALUATION

Some children who display symptoms of ADHD also appear to be anxious, depressed, or excessively angry. When these symptoms are severe, a psychiatric or psychological evaluation may be indicated. The purpose of this evaluation is to determine whether the child's anxiety, depression, or anger are causing or complicating his behavioral difficulties, or whether he is symptomatic as a result of his problems with attention, impulsivity, overactivity, school failure, and the like. Generally, when the psychological problems are complex, when the family is experiencing significant conflicts, or when alternative medications are indicated, a child psychiatrist is needed.

During the psychiatric evaluation, the child therapist will

explore with the child how he feels about himself, his family, his school situation, and his friends. He will inquire about the child's developmental milestones and medical history. He will observe the child's motor behavior, thought stream, ability to pay attention and concentrate, ability to engage in meaningful conversation, and overall mood. Usually the therapist will also want to assess the family history of learning and behavioral problems and the family's current situation, to determine how the child interacts with his parents and siblings and to determine the level of stress within the family. Sometimes the psychiatric evaluation will suggest that the entire family needs some sort of intervention. By the time some children come in for evaluation and treatment of ADHD, the parents have become so frustrated, angry, anxious, and depressed that they also need some support and understanding.

The first step in managing a child with ADHD usually involves gathering information through interviews, a physical exam, and rating scales, and by reviewing previous psychological testing. With this information, the care-provider should know if any further assessments are needed, if a medication trial is warranted, or if behavior therapy might be useful. The next step in managing the child is to implement and monitor the strategies chosen. These topics are discussed in the next three chapters.

CHAPTER 6

Medical Management

For many children with attentional or behavioral problems, the question of whether to medicate will come up sooner or later. Medication presents one of the most difficult dilemmas for parents. No one likes the idea of giving their children drugs, particularly when the drug of choice is one around which so much controversy rages. But at the same time, parents want what is best for their children—what will give them the best chance of achieving success in school and society. And so far, drugs are unquestionably effective for most children and appear to be the most effective single treatment approach.

The reluctance to medicate children stems in part from bad press that drugs such as Ritalin have gotten. In chapter 2, we briefly discussed the Ritalin controversy of the 1970s and the legal battles that continue even today. Every few months or so, an article appears in a popular magazine that criticizes the use of Ritalin for treating inattention and hyperactivity. As a result of Ritalin's negative public image, some pediatricians are reluctant to prescribe the drug and some parents are made to feel guilty if they consent to having their child medicated. Nevertheless, in 1990 an estimated 1 million children were medicated in order to control hyperactivity and inattention.

This is not to say that Ritalin is without its problems. It can be—and sometimes is—inappropriately prescribed. It can be —and sometimes is—abused. It can have negative side effects. It doesn't work for all children. Its effects are nonspecific, which means that it affects many aspects of brain function and not just those related to ADHD.

The purpose of this chapter is to describe what is and is not known about Ritalin as well as other drugs that are used to treat ADHD. For any drug to be effective and safe, it must be prescribed and monitored carefully. You need to know what benefits the drugs may have for your child and what the drugs will not do. You also need to know about possible side effects and how to recognize problems if they arise in your child.

In this book, we present several different treatment approaches for ADHD, but the mainstay of treatment is a multimodal combination of medication and behavior modification. So, you might ask, if behavior therapy is effective, why not use it instead of drugs? Unfortunately, some aspects of children's behavior are extremely difficult to modify. Moreover, there are definite limits as to what can be changed with medication. Medication will not make your child perfect; nor will it make him smarter. But what it can do is to relieve some of your child's difficulties so that he can tackle his problems more successfully.

Most of this chapter is devoted to Ritalin because it is the standard treatment against which all others are judged. It is also the most extensively researched and the most widely used. Indeed, the wide use of Ritalin partly explains why it comes under fire so frequently. Some of the other drugs that may be prescribed for your child do not carry the "baggage" of Ritalin; they are not so widely feared and mistrusted. But you should realize that they also have not been as extensively studied. None has proven to be as effective for as many children as has Ritalin, and none has been shown to be safer or better tolerated.

RITALIN AND OTHER STIMULANTS

Stimulants were first used to treat hyperactivity in 1937 by Charles Bradley, who used Benzedrine. In the 1960s Ritalin (methylphenidate) was developed and quickly became the most widely used treatment for what was then called hyperkinesis. Other commonly used stimulants include dextroamphetamine (Dexedrine) and pemoline (Cylert).

EFFECTS ON BEHAVIOR The idea of using a stimulant to treat hyperactivity may seem illogical. After all, according to the literature that accompanies stimulants, they are supposed to *increase,* not decrease motor activity. High doses of these drugs can indeed have a stimulating effect on normal individuals, giving them a "high" that may lead to abuse. But at the low doses prescribed by most physicians, these drugs enhance attention and thereby suppress overactivity. In addition, they increase mental alertness and the ability to focus and concentrate, while they reduce fatigue, brighten spirits, and sometimes produce a mild sense of euphoria. How they act to reduce overactivity and increase attention in children with ADHD is not fully understood. What is known, however, is that even non-ADHD children tend to become more attentive when given stimulants. Stimulants are thought to exert effects in several different areas of the brain and on different neurotransmitter systems.

Although the biochemical and physiological action of stimulants has been extensively studied, it is not clear how these physiological actions influence the symptoms of ADHD. But a lot is known about the overall behavioral effects of the drugs. In the classroom and at home, parents and teachers note that when children go on this medication, off-task activity levels decrease and the children become more compliant and less aggressive. Stimulants also seem to enhance self-control. Teachers often note that medicated children are better able to focus in on activities and stay "on task."

In other words, stimulants seem to help control the core problems of ADHD—hyperactivity, impulsivity, and inattentiveness. Laboratory testing supports this idea. For instance, on tests such as the Continuous Performance Test and the Paired Associate Learning Test (see chapter 5), which are supposed to assess children's ability to sustain attention, ADHD children's performance improves when they take stimulants, compared with their performance when unmedicated.

SECONDARY BENEFITS FROM BEHAVIOR IMPROVEMENT Making improvements in these behaviors appears to yield a number of secondary benefits. For one, children who are less aggressive and less impulsive tend to get along better with both their peers and their parents; stimulants may thereby break a repeating cycle of negative social interactions. Many children with ADHD get along poorly with their parents, for example. They tend to be oppositional and noncompliant, and the parents respond by being negative and punitive. But studies have shown that when children are treated with Ritalin, these conflicts become less severe; both the parents and the children's behavior improves. Researchers have shown by alternating the medication with a placebo that a child's improved behavior is not due simply to the parents' expectation that he will behave better on medication; rather that the child's improved behavior itself precipitates better parental behavior.

Although stimulants may improve the social behavior of children and thus their ability to make friends and get along with their peers, other steps are often necessary to bring about significant and long-lasting improvements in peer relationships. These steps are discussed in chapter 11.

EFFECTS ON LEARNING Ritalin is known to improve children's behavior in the classroom and elsewhere, but its effects on their learning processes are less clear. One might think that children would learn better and faster simply because they can pay better attention and require less frequent disciplining. But in several studies, children treated with stimulants still lagged behind in academic achievement. There are several possible explanations for this finding. Stimulants generally do little to rectify the cognitive difficulties that may affect children's ability to learn. For instance, if a child has difficulty processing things he hears (an auditory processing deficit), this difficulty will probably remain even when his inattentiveness is controlled. For the large proportion of ADHD children who have learning difficulties, stimulants treat only part of their problem.

Another reason that studies have failed to show learning benefits resulting from stimulant treatment is that learning benefits may be subtle and not measurable except over a fairly long time period. For example, assume a child starts taking Ritalin in the middle of the school year, at which time he is performing below grade level. He takes Ritalin through the end of the school year. Even though he may experience some academic benefits as a result of the medication, he will most likely still be below grade level at the end of the year. Recent research has shown that medication contributes to substantial improvements on specific academic tasks such as math and spelling. But the tests commonly used to assess achievement may not be sensitive enough to catch modest improvements, even though these improvements may be significant over time.

A third possible reason for the lack of clear learning benefits is that the behavioral improvements that do result from the medication are simply insufficient to make up for the years of school underachievement that children experience before medication. For example, a child who begins taking Ritalin in fourth grade may have already missed learning some of the primary skills necessary for success later in life. In addition, he may have already begun to identify himself as a failure and may be unable to shake the negative emotional baggage he has gathered over the years. This line of reasoning argues strongly for early intervention in children with ADHD.

Some researchers have suggested that Ritalin may negatively affect learning by causing children to "overfocus," which presumably limits their flexible or creative thinking. This could explain why medicated children do better on highly structured tests of attention and vigilance yet still do not perform better in school. Studies have been designed to test this hypothesis, using a variety of tools to test different aspects of cognitive function, such as flexibility and problem-solving ability. But the results have been inconsistent. In a few studies, Ritalin seemed to decrease performance on these tests, while in other studies no such effect was seen. In still other studies, Ritalin was observed to increase children's performance on these more complex learning tasks.

In short, the effect of Ritalin on learning is not clear, but it appears to be relatively mild over the short term. Some researchers believe that over time, the benefits could be substantial. Nevertheless, if your child has learning difficulties, types of intervention besides Ritalin will likely be necessary to help him.

SIDE EFFECTS OF STIMULANT THERAPY The side effects that result from taking Ritalin can be divided into three general groups: those that are common, those that are rare, and those that are extremely rare.

Common side effects are those that are experienced by many children. If they are going to appear, they usually appear at the beginning of treatment. Common side effects include *gastrointestinal disturbances,* such as decreased appetite or an upset stomach. Your child might say to you, "My stomach doesn't feel good." Usually, the feeling they describe is not nausea, although younger children may say they feel sick to their stomachs. These complaints usually last for no more than a week and are not affected by whether the child takes the medication before or after meals.

Appetite suppression effects are another common side effect.

They may be less noticeable if the drugs are taken after meals, as the effects usually wear off before the next meal. Despite the appetite suppression, medicated children generally do not lose weight or fail to gain weight to a significant degree. This may be because medicated children are less active and therefore are burning fewer calories, or because they adjust their eating schedules to accommodate times when they aren't hungry. Parents can help lessen the importance of appetite suppression effects by being flexible about eating times. In addition, the child's growth should be monitored closely.

Other common side effects include *insomnia* and *headaches,* which may occur either while the medicine is in effect or when it is wearing off. If a child gets a headache right after taking the medicine, he may be taking too high a dose. Late-in-the-day headaches are more common and should be monitored closely. If they persist for some time or are severe, your doctor may want to adjust the medication program.

Children taking stimulants may also experience *a slight increase in heart rate or blood pressure,* which is usually of little concern. Nonetheless, it should be monitored. It may present a problem for adolescents who have a family history of heart disease. Some children also report feeling *jittery,* which may be related to taking the medication on an empty stomach.

A final common side effect that is less understood is the problem of *rebound.* Rebound is a worsening of certain behavioral symptoms after a medication has worn off. Many parents report that after the medication wears off, their children do not simply go "back to normal" but are actually worse than before they took the drug. They seem to have a shorter fuse, and they tend to tantrum, cry, and get angry more easily. Some parents say their children become hypertalkative or hyperactive. These effects typically last for an hour at most after the medication wears off, but nevertheless they can be bothersome.

Less common side effects include growth suppression and tics. *Growth suppression* usually does not become a problem because children tend to make up for any growth delays caused by medication during "medication vacations." These are time periods during the summer or part of the summer when your doctor may recommend that the child refrain from taking the drug (see below). By closely monitoring your child's growth, you can catch any growth inhibition before it becomes a problem.

Tics are stereotyped repetitive behaviors, such as facial blinks. Most tics are benign and transient, and they occur frequently during childhood. But stimulants may bring out more complex tic disorders such as Tourette syndrome in children who are predisposed to them.

Extremely rare side effects related to long-term medication include a serious condition called *bone marrow suppression,* which can cause anemia and other blood-related problems. This side effect is so rare that most physicians do not routinely order laboratory blood analyses for it unless there is some prior indication of a problem. If your child has a related condition such as a blood disorder or liver disease, however, your doctor may elect to monitor blood tests more carefully or not use medication at all.

Despite all the controversy over the dangers of Ritalin therapy, few studies have specifically looked at the incidence of its various side effects. However, one recent study did just that.[7] The physical and behavioral characteristics of eighty-three children were assessed under three different medication conditions: a placebo, a low dose of Ritalin, and a high dose of Ritalin. The trial was designed so that neither the children nor their parents knew which dose the children were taking at any given time. As was expected, the most common side effects the children experienced were decreased appetite, insomnia, stomachaches, and headaches. In fact, these were the only side effects for which significant differences were observed when Ritalin was compared with a placebo. Some of the other behavioral characteristics that have been attributed to side effects of Ritalin therapy, such as anxiousness, irritability, sadness, and blank staring, occurred just as frequently when the children received the placebo as when they received Ritalin. Only three children experienced side effects serious enough to warrant discontinuation of the drug, and these side effects all disappeared quickly when the drug was withdrawn.

This study supports the widely held view that stimulants are relatively safe but that adverse reactions and significant side effects can occur. You can protect your child by making sure that both you and your doctor are closely monitoring side effects as well as effectiveness. Most of the serious side effects, if they are going to show up, show up early and will disappear quickly if the drug is withdrawn. If your child experiences mild side effects, such as mild headaches or stomachaches, your doctor may suggest that you continue the medication for a week or two and pay close attention to how the child feels. Some of these mild side effects will disappear in the first few weeks. If they don't, another drug—even another stimulant—may be better tolerated.

CONTRAINDICATIONS: WHO SHOULD NOT TAKE RITALIN? For some children, Ritalin therapy may be best avoided. One of the main objectives of the physical exam is to determine whether your child is one of these children. Liver disease, certain forms of heart disease, and high blood pressure are the clearest contraindications to Ritalin therapy. Stimulants may also be ruled out for children with seizure disorders, as the drug can theoretically lower the seizure threshold and thus increase the likelihood of seizures. Doctors sometimes decide to try medicating such children with an anticonvulsant and a stimulant simultaneously. Preliminary studies suggest that when children's seizures are under good control with anticonvulsant medication, adding a stimulant may enhance their attention without increasing the risk of seizures.

Stimulants are also generally avoided in patients who have tic disorders, including Tourette syndrome. But tics often do not appear until a child is over age seven, by which time he may already have undergone a few years of stimulant treatment. Thus, doctors generally use stimulants cautiously in children who have a family history of tics, because stimulants are thought to increase the likelihood of tics developing or worsen them. However, some studies have indicated that stimulants do not worsen tics and that these drugs can be used safely in ADHD children with tics.

Stimulants are also thought to aggravate anxiety. In a child who has ADHD and is anxious as well, an alternative to stimulant medication may be chosen.

If your child is taking stimulants, your doctor will want you to avoid mixing them with other drugs that affect behavior, including antidepressants, sedatives, sleeping pills, and over-the-counter cold preparations that contain ephedrine or pseudoephedrine. If your child has a cold, you may be able to give him cold medicine at night after the Ritalin has worn off or on days when he stays home from school and doesn't need to take Ritalin. Reinforce to your child that stimulants can be dangerous if too much is taken. If the drug works and helps him to function better, tell him that it will not work better to take more. Older children may be able to take responsibility for taking their medication, but parents should dispense the drug carefully to young children.

DOSAGE: HOW OFTEN AND HOW MUCH? Regular-release (short-acting) Ritalin affects behavior quickly and wears off in a short time. Its effects usually last no longer than three to six hours. Another formulation, called extended- or sustained-release Ritalin, (Ritalin-SR) is also available; its effects last for approximately eight hours.

Individual reactions to Ritalin vary widely, and this affects the dosage. For some children, one 5 mg tablet in the morning is a sufficient dose, while for others, a 10, 15, or 20 mg dose up to three times per day may be required. Some children don't respond to the drug at all, although the percentage of Ritalin nonresponders is unknown. Published reports suggest that an adequate response can be obtained in 70 to 80 percent of children, leaving 20 to 30 percent as nonresponders. But in the clinic at The Children's Hospital of Philadelphia and its affiliates, the percentage of nonresponders appears to be lower. This difference may reflect the different criteria that people use to determine whether a child is a responder or a nonresponder; or it may represent a different subpopulation of children that are treated in this particular clinic. It may also be that some children are classified as nonresponders when they actually have not received an appropriate dose of the drug. Whatever the reason, it is clear that not all children respond to Ritalin.

There are two important points to keep in mind with regard to Ritalin responsiveness. First, whether a child responds or not says nothing about whether he truly has ADHD. Even normal children with no problems of hyperactivity or inattentiveness often become more attentive and focused when given stimulants. Second, the fact that a particular child does not respond to Ritalin does not mean that he will not respond to a different stimulant. Each of the three commonly used stimulants—Ritalin, Dexedrine, and Cylert —acts by a somewhat different mechanism and affects individual children differently.

Whether a child is classified as a responder or a nonresponder depends to some extent on the criteria one uses to judge response and the source from which information is obtained. Parent and/or teacher reports of children's behavior are often used to evaluate their responsiveness. Although these reports may provide important information, they are subject to the personal opinions of the evaluator. A teacher, for example, may report that a child's behavior is still below expectations even though it has greatly improved. At a higher dose, the teacher may judge the behavior improvement to be adequate, but the child may experience some unwanted side effects.

This concept was graphically illustrated in a 1977 study that looked at how different doses of Ritalin affect teacher ratings of children's behavior, heart rate, and the ability to perform academic tasks.[8] In this study, children who received low doses of Ritalin performed well on an academic task but still received low teacher ratings for behavior. Their heart rate was not affected. At the high dose, however, teachers rated the children's behavior as greatly improved, while their academic performance fell substantially. This study was taken to mean that academic performance had to be sacrificed in order to achieve adequate behavior control. But subsequent studies revealed that the levels of Ritalin used in the 1977 study were too extreme. At a dose higher than the low dose but lower than the high dose, a balance could be achieved at which both behavior and learning were optimal. What you want to strive for is the lowest dosage at which your child's behavior is adequately improved but at which side effects are minimized.

Determining the appropriate dosage of Ritalin often takes some experimentation. Studies report that effective dosages range from 0.3 to 1.5 mg per kilogram of body weight per day (mg/kg/day), up to a maximum of 60 mg/day. This means that for a 60-pound (27.3 kg) child, the effective dose could range between 10 mg/day and 40 mg/day. The actual appropriate dosage must be individualized for each child. Because Ritalin acts so quickly, the effectiveness of a particular dose can be evaluated in a relatively short time. This means that your doctor can set up a medication trial in which several different dosages are tried over a period of two to four weeks. Such a trial was conducted for Alex, the ten-year-old boy you met in the introduction. Alex's parents, though initially reluctant to medicate, decided to try stimulants after behavior intervention improved his level of functioning but still did not bring him to the level he appeared capable of reaching (see box).

Alex

Alex's trial was set up over a four-week period. Before the evaluation began, his teachers were asked to fill out "daily report" forms (see chapter 7) that assessed his behavior and attentiveness in class. These daily reports were used as baseline information from which later comparisons could be made. On each day of the trial except Sunday, Alex received one of four doses of Ritalin (0, 5, 10, or 15 mg). The doses were given in random order, and the teachers were not told which dose Alex was receiving on a particular day. Each day, the teachers filled out a daily report form. After the first few days at the 15 mg dose, Alex's teachers reported that he cried frequently and complained of headaches. Therefore, the 15 mg dose was dropped from the trial. At the end of the trial, all the daily reports were collected and compared to the dose of medication that Alex received. This allowed Alex's doctor to see the effects of the different doses of medication on his behavior. In addition, by giving a dose on Saturday, Alex's parents were able to observe his behavior on medication at home.

In Alex's case, the lowest dose of medication (5 mg) brought about a significant improvement in his behavior that was not substantially improved at higher doses. He subsequently began taking 5 mg of Ritalin a day every morning before school.

Not all drug trials yield results as dramatic and clear-cut as Alex's. Sometimes a trial of an even higher dose is necessary. Sometimes the drug produces side effects before adequate behavior control is achieved. And sometimes the drug proves ineffective at any dose, in which case another drug may be tried.

For example, five-year-old Nate was given 10 mg of Ritalin because he was extremely overactive. The drug appeared to help a little, but not enough for him to get along either in school or at home. Every month his pediatrician increased the dosage by a little bit, until he reached the maximum of 60 mg/day: 30 mg in the morning and 30 mg at lunchtime. Six months after Nate started taking the medicine, his mother noticed that he was biting his fingers and lips and grimacing more than usual. She brought him to The Children's Hospital of Philadelphia for an evaluation. Even though his behavior was still not in control, the doctors decided to withdraw the medication because he appeared to be a poor responder and to suffer significant side effects. After that, they shifted Nate to an alternative drug.

Medication trials for other drugs are structured differently in order to account for the different characteristics of each drug, such as how long it takes to become effective and how long its effects last. These characteristics are discussed below.

One dose of Ritalin in the morning is sufficient to carry some children through for the entire day. More often, however, children need at least two doses per day and possibly a third. Typically, doses are given at breakfast and lunchtime. Older children may be entrusted to take the drug on their own at lunchtime; if not, a school nurse or teacher may be asked to dispense the medication. Whether a child needs a late-afternoon dose depends on many factors, including the child's at-home behavior, the amount and difficulty of homework he receives, and the after-school activities in which he may participate. Sometimes an afternoon dose is indicated but is found to cause sleep problems. In such cases, the doctor may suggest adjusting the time at which the child takes the afternoon dose. Sometimes the sleep difficulties appear to be caused not by the stimulating effects of the drug but by rebound; in these cases, the doctor may recommend that the child take a small dose of medication closer to bedtime. Many people feel that Ritalin is for school only and that parents should be able to handle children at home without medication. But this may not always be in a child's best interests. If his behavior adds significant stress to the family or if he is unable to concentrate on his homework, withholding medication may do a child more harm than good.

An alternative is sustained-release Ritalin, which can be given as a single dose once in the morning, and supplemented with a late-afternoon dose of regular-release Ritalin if necessary. Though this regimen works for some children, it tends to be somewhat less effective for the majority, since in some children the absorption is erratic.

Once an effective dosage has been determined for your child, you must decide, in consultation with your doctor, whether he will take the medicine on weekends and during school vacations. Many parents feel that their children need the drugs mainly to help them sustain attention in the classroom and that outside school they function well. For other children, however, extracurricular activities may pose problems. If a child plays baseball, for example, he may have difficulty if he cannot pay attention to the game. Fourteen-year-old Caroline ran on her school's track team. She usually took Ritalin only on school days. But sometimes track meets were held on Saturdays. She found that she was better able to concentrate on the meet and maintain her composure if she took her medication on those days as well. Each child's situation must be evaluated separately to determine what will benefit him the most.

A similar decision must be made with respect to medicating a child over school breaks and holidays. Usually doctors suggest that children go drug-free for at least some period during summer vacation. This allows them to catch up on any growth delays they may have experienced, and it allows parents to observe whether their needs for medication have changed. Some children "outgrow" the behaviors that led to their medication in the first place. If you and your doctor do decide to give your child a medication vacation, you need not do it for the entire summer if the child or your family has planned activities that require a high level of cooperation and compliance. For example, if your child is going to a summer day camp, the medication may help him to build better friendships with the other children and participate more fully in camp activities.

LONG-TERM USE OF RITALIN Since ADHD is a long-term condition, medical treatment may be required for a prolonged period of time. This raises at least two concerns for many parents: First, will the child become tolerant of the medication? Second, will he become addicted? The answers to both these questions appears to be no, although further studies of long-term treatment are needed before definitive answers can be given. Over time, children's Ritalin dosages may need to be increased, but at least one study has suggested that the amount of increase needed relates more to children's increased body weight than to their becoming tolerant of a certain dose. Some children, but not most, may become tolerant of Ritalin. Therefore, your doctor should continue to monitor its effectiveness. Addiction to Ritalin appears to occur very infrequently. More often, when children get to be teenagers, they refuse to take the medication, wanting more to be like their friends. Several studies have suggested that alcoholism and drug abuse occur more frequently among people with ADHD than among "normal" people, but this does not appear to be related to whether the person took Ritalin.

Some people feel that the long-term use of Ritalin or any medication may have negative implications for children's self-esteem. Children who are medicated for a long time may internalize a sense that they are abnormal or bad, or they may avoid taking responsibility for their actions and blame their problems on the medication. (These issues are discussed in chapter 11.)

Although ADHD-related problems may persist throughout a child's life, his need for medication may diminish. Frequently, when children reach adolescence, doctors suggest stopping the medication. Still, some children continue to require medication throughout their teenage years and even into adulthood. Few studies have assessed the long-term health implications of prolonged Ritalin use. Until more studies are done, children will have to be monitored closely to make sure their health remains optimal.

DEXEDRINE AND PEMOLINE Much of the information regarding Ritalin also pertains to the other commonly used stimulants: dextro-amphetamine (Dexedrine) and pemoline (Cylert). These two stimulants have slightly different modes of action and may affect different neurotransmitter systems to different degrees. Thus, one stimulant may work better than another for a particular child. But Ritalin appears to be effective for the most children, and since Ritalin has been widely used for many years, much more is known about its safety profile.

The side effects associated with Dexedrine are similar to those associated with Ritalin, except that they occur more frequently. The usual dosage ranges between 0.15 and 0.4 mg/kg/day. Like Ritalin, Dexedrine often requires twice-daily dosing, and its effects can be seen within the first hour or so. Dexedrine is also available in a sustained-release form.

Cylert has been used more extensively in Europe than in the United States. It differs from the other stimulants primarily in the timing of its action. With Ritalin, the blood levels of the drug fall quickly and its effectiveness wears off in three to four hours. But with Cylert, the blood levels remain high for longer, and its effectiveness does not begin to wear off for about seven hours. Although it remains effective for longer, twice-daily dosing may still be necessary. Cylert's advantage is that the second dose may be given after school, so that parents can dispense it rather than rely on the school nurse. Cylert also offers the advantage that with twice-daily dosing, blood levels remain fairly consistent rather than fluctuating up and down significantly, as they do with Ritalin and Dexedrine. Thus, rebound does not occur.

One potential disadvantage of Cylert is that its effectiveness sometimes builds up gradually over the first two to three weeks of therapy, necessitating a medication trial that lasts several weeks or months rather than several days. Some investigators now dispute this contention, however, and say that Cylert's effectiveness can be assessed by the second or third day of medication. The usual starting dose is 37.5 mg/day, given in the morning. This dose can be gradually increased to 112.5 mg/day. Its common side effects are similar to those associated with Ritalin. Toxicity to the liver may also occur.

ANTIDEPRESSANTS

When stimulants don't work, when they produce unwanted side effects, or when a child has a coexisting condition that precludes the use of stimulants, an alternative drug may be used. In recent years, tricyclic antidepressants (TCAs) have gained popularity in the treatment of ADHD, particularly in adolescents and adults who are also depressed. The most commonly used TCAs are imipramine (trade name Tofranil or Janimine) and desipramine (trade name Norpramin or Pertofrane). These drugs offer several possible advantages over stimulants. For one, they have a longer duration of action and therefore can be given either once or twice a day so that they maintain a consistent blood level; this lessens the risk of rebound. Another advantage is that they carry with them a low risk of abuse or dependency; and they may be less likely to cause a worsening of anxiety or depression if those conditions coexist with ADHD. Finally, they appear less likely to worsen tics or suppress appetite.

But TCAs have disadvantages as well. Most important, there have been several recent reports of sudden death in children who took desipramine for either ADHD or bedwetting. Whether other TCAs besides desipramine also increase the risk of sudden death is unknown. Clearly, more research needs to be done before TCAs can be considered safe for children with ADHD. At this time, there is no universal agreement about the use of TCAs in people with ADHD. (Their side effects and precautionary measures are discussed more fully below.)

TCAs work by a mechanism of action different from that of stimulants, although the exact mechanism remains unclear. Like stimulants, TCAs interact with neurotransmitters. Desipramine appears to act on a specific neurotransmitter called norepinephrine, and it therefore may be associated with fewer adverse reactions than drugs that act on many neurotransmitters. In children with ADHD, its behavioral effects are similar to those in children who take stimulants. In one recent study, desipramine was judged as significantly improving behavior in nearly 70 percent of patients, compared with about 10 percent of patients who received a placebo. TCAs may also bring about a general improvement in children's moods.

The effects of TCAs on learning are less clear. On laboratory tests of cognitive function, children taking TCAs have shown little or no improvement. But there may be long-term learning benefits that have not yet been studied, as there were with the early studies of Ritalin's effects.

SIDE EFFECTS Like stimulants, TCAs may produce a number of common but relatively minor side effects. These include dry mouth, decreased appetite, headaches, stomach pain, fatigue, dizziness, and trouble sleeping. TCAs are also associated with blood pressure elevations, changes in heart rate, and rhythm abnormalities. In most studies, these changes were judged to be significant but clinically unimportant. But in light of the recent reports of sudden death in children taking desipramine, the importance of changes in heart function needs to be reevaluated. Sudden death occurs when the heart suddenly and unexpectedly begins to beat extremely fast. Unfortunately, there is no easy method for determining who is predisposed to fatal rhythm abnormalities. Therefore, children who suffer from heart abnormalities or who have a family history of sudden death may be eliminated from consideration for taking TCAs.

The sudden deaths occurred in eight- to ten-year-old boys, even though TCAs have been approved by the FDA for use only in adolescents and adults. Therefore, many physicians may avoid TCA medication for children under twelve until more is known about how to prevent the occurrence of sudden death. But TCA use in adolescents and adults appears to be relatively safe.

When TCAs are prescribed for ADHD, they are usually started at a fairly low dose, then gradually increased until adequate behavior control is achieved. For desipramine, this level is usually about 4.5 mg/kg/day. Doses lower than 3.5 mg/kg/day have been found to be less effective, and doses higher than 5 mg/kg/day have been associated with worsening side effects. High doses of imipramine have been noted to cause nightmares, agitation, muscle pain, and irritability, among other complications.

Little is known about the long-term use of TCAs. They have been widely used to treat depression in both adolescents and adults, but such treatment usually lasts for only three to six months at a time. Currently, it is not known whether any long-term adverse effects are associated with TCA use or whether tolerance to the drug develops. In several studies, imipramine's effectiveness appeared to diminish over time, and in some cases it has actually been associated with a worsening of symptoms. Since TCAs do not give patients the feeling of euphoria or the "high" sometimes associated with stimulant use in adults, the risk of abuse appears to be insignificant.

CLONIDINE

In recent years, the antihypertensive drug clonidine (trade name Catapres) has been gaining favor as an alternative treatment for ADHD. The use of clonidine in children has not been studied extensively, but early reports suggest that it may be effective in ADHD children who have frequent temper tantrums, a short fuse, and excessive anger, or when stimulants produce too many side effects. It may also be helpful in ADHD patients who are anxious or depressed. But it does not appear to be powerful in influencing the core symptoms of ADHD. One study found substantial behavioral improvement in 50 percent of children with ADHD and moderate improvement in another 25 percent.

Clonidine acts by a completely different mechanism from stimulants and antidepressants. But again, how it acts to modify behavior in children with ADHD is unknown. It appears to increase calmness and attention and may also reduce anxiety. Its effects on learning have not been well studied.

When children are given clonidine for ADHD, doctors generally start with a low dosage and gradually increase it up to 4 or 5 mcg/kg/day, given in divided doses four times a day. If your child is given clonidine, you cannot reliably assess its effectiveness for some time. After about one month, clinical effects can be seen but maximum effectiveness may not be evident for two to three months. The most common side effect is sleepiness; other common side effects include dry mouth and nausea. The drug commonly produces a drop in blood pressure, so blood pressure should be monitored carefully at the beginning of treatment. If clonidine is judged to be ineffective, the drug must be withdrawn gradually to avoid any abrupt changes in blood pressure.

OTHER MEDICATIONS

Other drugs that are sometimes used to treat ADHD include newer antidepressants such as fluoxetine and burproprion; a group of antidepressants called monoamine oxidase (MAO) inhibitors; lithium, which is generally used to treat bipolar disorder (manic-depressive illness); and the anticonvulsant carbamazepine (trade name Tegretol). None of these has been extensively studied in children with ADHD. But if your child does not respond to other treatment methods, your physician may recommend a trial with one of these drugs.

Sometimes doctors recommend using two or more drugs simultaneously. This approach is usually reserved for children who have more than one problem, such as ADHD and anxiety, ADHD and depression, or ADHD and a conduct disorder. Whenever multiple drugs are used, doctors must be especially careful to monitor children for side effects and possible drug interactions.

■ ■ ■

To sum up: the management of ADHD often involves stimulant medication. Ritalin, the most commonly used stimulant, has been used extensively for nearly thirty years and still appears to be the most effective and least toxic drug available. But you should be aware that drugs will not solve all your child's problems. In addition, you should make sure that your child is given an appropriate dosage of medication and that he is monitored carefully throughout his treatment. With those precautions, you can help ensure that your child will not suffer serious side effects.

CHAPTER 7

Behavior Management

Despite its effectiveness in many aspects of treatment for children with ADHD, medication has its limitations. Many studies have suggested that medication as the sole form of treatment does not confer long-term benefits to ADHD children because it does not help them significantly in their social and academic functioning. Thus, behavioral approaches to therapy may be needed in order to tackle behavioral difficulties associated with ADHD.

Indeed, although children with ADHD have different combinations of strengths and weaknesses, many if not most could benefit from some sort of behavioral intervention. Some children with ADHD benefit from intervention that is quite intense. For example, when a child's refusal to follow rules or comply with parental or teacher requests has resulted in suspension from school, a breakdown in the family's ability to function, or danger to himself or others, behavior therapy may be needed to set up a management program tailored specifically to meet that child's needs. Other children with ADHD benefit from much milder behavioral interventions. Not all children with ADHD present "behavior problems" to their parents or teachers in the sense of causing disruptions, getting into fights with other children, and throwing temper tantrums. But their more passive behaviors, such as daydreaming or forgetting things, cause them significant problems, such as lack of productivity. These can sometimes be rectified with behavioral interventions.

The term *behavior intervention* is used generically to describe any kind of intervention that is geared to change behavior. *Behavior management* refers to more systematic approaches that parents or teachers might use to influence behavior. *Behavior therapy* involves seeking professional help in setting up a behavior management program.

Studies of the effectiveness of behavior therapy have yielded inconsistent results. When behavior therapy is used as the sole form of treatment, the benefits realized generally fall short of the benefits realized with stimulant therapy. This may be partly because effective behavior-management programs are difficult to implement. They require ongoing efforts and cooperation over long periods of time by the children, parents, and teachers if they are to work.

Thus, while medication and behavior therapy used alone often have shortcomings, when used together the two treatment modalities can complement each other. This was seen dramatically in the case of our friend Alex. The initial behavioral approach to his treatment instilled a sense of confidence and hope in him, and a subsequent low dose of medication increased his ability to focus and maintain control. The multimodal combination led to dramatic improvement in his classroom behavior, his ability to complete homework, and his relationships with his family members.

WHAT IS BEHAVIOR MANAGEMENT?

The term *behavior management* refers to a number of techniques that are designed to change or eliminate undesirable behaviors and increase wanted behaviors through the use of rewards, skills training, and environmental manipulation. Depending on the nature of a particular child's difficulties, behavior therapists use any of several techniques. Some are easier to implement than others; some require a great deal of cooperation on the part of the child's teachers; some require extreme amounts of vigilance on the part of the parents.

Before you begin a behavior-management program for your child, you will want to identify specific behaviors that need changing. Make sure that you have chosen behaviors, which can be changed, rather than temperamental characteristics, which are relatively stable. For instance, you cannot behaviorally modify your child's short attention span, but you may be able to teach him strategies for staying on task and completing activities. Try to establish realistic expectations for a behavior-management program. If your child has difficulty staying seated in class, for example, you may not be able to achieve the goal of having him stay in his seat for an entire class period. But you and his teachers might accept a lessening of his overactivity, combined with some other techniques that will reduce the impact of his behavior on the rest of the class and help him benefit from classwork. One teacher assigned a child with ADHD two seats and told him that when he felt the need to get up and move, he could switch from one seat to the other. This strategy provided him with an outlet for his energy that didn't involve breaking rules and that allowed him to remain in the classroom, and it alleviated the teacher's need to constantly discipline him.

This teacher was obviously highly motivated to help the child, and she was flexible in her approach. When you begin a behavior-management program, you need to assess the amount of support you can expect to receive from teachers and others who deal with your child. At the end of this chapter, we discuss strategies for establishing a good working relationship with your child's teachers.

Finally, you need to determine if you yourself are ready to work on a behavior-management program. Behavior-management programs are difficult to implement unless parents are well prepared mentally and emotionally. If both the mother and the father are helping to raise the child, they must be willing to work together, to be consistent, and to help each other. When there are other conflicts within the family that hinder a good working relationship, the family may need counseling or psychotherapy to help resolve those conflicts first (see chapter 9). Before you start on a behavior-management program, you should understand what will be expected of you and what you can expect from the program.

PARENT TRAINING: BEHAVIOR THERAPY AT HOME

One of the most frequent complaints heard from parents of children with ADHD is that the children won't do what they're told. Sometimes it is not clear whether the children actually hear parental instructions or if they have simply learned to "tune out" their parents' voices. Some children seem to disobey as a way of getting attention. Many parents establish techniques for effectively dealing with noncompliant children on their own, but even the most highly skilled parents sometimes need help with ADHD children. These children are limit-testers and system-debuggers; they find loopholes in any rule established, and they consistently find ways to undermine the system.

Parents trying to raise a child with ADHD—or any difficult child, for that matter—often get locked into patterns that increase the likelihood of their child's noncompliance. These patterns establish a climate of negative interactions between parent and child and affect the entire family. Some parents (especially mothers) become depressed or overstressed and develop low self-esteem; marriages become strained; and siblings become angry. Other parents (especially fathers) are at risk for alcohol and substance abuse. In addition, noncompliant behavior in children is strongly associated with future conduct problems in adolescence and young adulthood.

Parent training teaches parents behavior-management techniques that they can implement at home. It can help parents who feel that their own systems have not worked as well as they would like. It teaches parents to focus not just on the child but on family interactions as well, thereby helping parents unlock themselves from destructive patterns.

Parent training takes a number of different forms. Several books are available that outline different approaches to developing effective skills to manage children's behavior.[9] Parents may also learn techniques through one-on-one counseling with a behavior therapist, such as a psychologist, psychiatrist, or social worker. A third option is to attend a class that teaches parenting skills in a structured program. Such classes may be found at community centers, schools, or child-care centers; they are also offered through hospital-based clinics and doctors' offices. The Philadelphia ADHD Clinic offers a parent-training program geared specifically to parents of children with ADHD.*

In this chapter, we briefly describe the Philadelphia program, which involves discussion, role-playing, and homework assignments. This description is not meant to be a "how-to" program that you would implement at home. But it may give you insight into the basis of the difficulties you are having at home and whether you might benefit from attending a parent-training program.

BREAKING THE CYCLE THAT PERPETUATES NONCOMPLIANCE Patterns of noncompliance often begin when a parent issues a command to do a task, and the child either ignores it or refuses to comply. The parent repeats the command, and the child continues to refuse. This cycle may be repeated several times, and the parent becomes more and more frustrated with each request. The parent may then turn to threats: "If you don't pick up those toys, I'm going to spank you!" Such threats still may not convince the child to comply, which leads the parent to repeat this cycle a few times. Finally, in anger and frustration, the parent may resort to punishing the child. At this point, the child still may or may not comply, but either way he has successfully delayed doing the task at hand. In addition, he has gotten a lot of attention from the parent, so he is

* The program is based loosely on the program developed by Russell Barkley in *Defiant Children: A Clinician's Manual for Parent Training* (New York: The Guilford Press, 1987).

likely to repeat the pattern again. The next time a similar issue arises, the parent may refrain from setting or trying to enforce a limit, wishing to avoid a repeat of the conflict.

The goal of parent training is to prevent parents from getting stuck in this pattern. In order to accomplish this goal, parents must understand why children misbehave and some basic principles of child management. For parents to be effective, they must be firm, consistent, and clear when they give directions. Children must understand exactly what is expected of them and what the consequences are for noncompliance. Those consequences must be delivered consistently when rules are broken, no matter what the circumstances. Consequences are usually most effective when they are delivered immediately after the noncompliance; likewise, when praise is appropriate, it should be given immediately. Both parents must reinforce the consequences—otherwise, enforcement of the rules is much less effective, and marital conflict may even arise.

When these general principles of child management are understood, parents are ready to begin a step-by-step program that will help them restructure their family relationships and establish better ways of interacting. Each step can be difficult, and sometimes interactions appear to get worse before they begin to improve. One of the advantages of a parent-training class is that parents can share their experiences and learn from one another. When a parent is becoming discouraged and considering quitting, other parents in similar situations, as well as the teacher or leader of the class, can lend needed support.

GIVING POSITIVE ATTENTION Frequently, difficult children are trying to get attention in mostly negative ways. Thus, the next step in parent training is for parents to find ways to give their child more positive attention. In essence, parent training trains you to act as a play therapist. This means learning to pay closer attention to your child, to notice carefully and appreciate what he is doing, and to play with him in a meaningful way, letting him take the lead in your play. Parent training teaches you to "catch him being good," while trying to ignore, as much as you can, the behaviors you wish to eliminate. Ignoring misbehavior can be one of the most difficult parts of the program, but frequently children stop the misbehavior when it is no longer drawing attention—although it sometimes takes a while for them to do so. Some misbehaviors cannot be ignored, of course, such as hitting a little sister or breaking things in the house. When parents must intervene, they should try to remove the child from the situation in a straightforward and firm manner, remove the privilege the child is enjoying or is about to enjoy, and refrain as much as possible from giving him attention in the form of lectures or arguments.

In parent training, after the parent has practiced giving the child positive attention, he is ready to begin making requests and encouraging compliance through praise and appreciation. Parents' expectations must be made clear and should be issued as commands or simple statements rather than as questions. "You need to hang up your jacket" is more likely to work than "Would you please hang up your jacket?" Children with ADHD often take longer than other children to realize and internalize parents' expectations, so they may need more external support. Start small. For instance, at first you may want to hand the child the jacket before you issue the command "You need to hang up your jacket." No matter how small the task, if the child complies, he should be acknowledged and praised: "Good job hanging up your jacket." Frequently, ADHD children are not used to hearing praise, and the parents are not used to praising them. Such parents must make an extra effort to find circumstances for praise.

ENCOURAGING APPROPRIATE BEHAVIOR AND INDEPENDENT PLAY The next aspect of parent training focuses on decreasing the child's frequent demands for attention. Attention-seeking behavior can be particularly disruptive if it occurs while a parent is trying to do something else. For instance, some children seem to demand attention immediately after Mom picks up the phone or begins speaking to a friend. In order to discourage disruptions and encourage independent play, parent training instructs parents to be aware of times when the child is not interrupting and to give him attention at those times. In addition, parents should try to "shape" the child's behavior by setting up situations in which they can encourage noninterruption in small steps. For example, a mother begins a telephone conversation while the child is playing independently. Before the child has a chance to interrupt, the mother might stop her conversation momentarily and check in on the child, giving him some attention and acknowledging his ability to play on his own. Then the mother returns to her phone conversation. Periodically and at ever-lengthening intervals, she continues to pause in her conversation and give her child attention, thus increasing the amount of time that the child is able to play independently.

ADDING INCENTIVES   Usually, praise and positive reinforcement alone are not enough to change a child's noncompliant behavior. These reinforcers, however, lay the groundwork for more concrete motivators. The next level of parent training is to encourage compliance by using concrete rewards and incentives. Such rewards may be poker chips or points that can be cashed in for privileges. Children earn the chips or points when they comply with rules, demands, or chores, and they use the chips to earn a variety of desirable activities or things. In order to implement a successful incentive system, parents and children are encouraged to develop their list of demands and rewards together. For instance, a child may earn points for remembering to bring things home from school, for hanging up his jacket, or for doing his homework. Some items on the list of demands should be things that will be easy for the child to do; other items should require more effort. The list of rewards should include items that are both desirable to the child and reasonable for the parents. Daily as well as weekly rewards should be included on the list. Daily rewards allow the child to see the benefits of his compliance quickly, while weekly rewards encourage longer-lasting behavioral changes and allow the child to work toward something more substantial and thus more motivating. In order to realize the benefits of both daily and weekly rewards, some parents require the child to spend at least one chip daily but allow him to bank the rest until he has accumulated enough for a weekly reward. Social rewards, such as a special outing with Mom or Dad, often have greater impact than do material rewards. (For an example of these lists, see box.)

Luke's Point System

This is the point system that seven-year-old Luke and his parents worked out. After coming up with the list of rewards, they agreed that Luke should be able to earn a minimum of 4 points each day. He was allowed to "bank" any points over 4 that he received in one day in order to save for a special treat on the weekend.

Luke earns points if he:

- Gets up by 7:00 A.M. without Mom's help (1 point)
- Makes his bed (2 points)
- Catches the bus on time (1 point)
- Remembers his books and papers from school (1 point)
- Hangs up his jacket when he comes home (1 point)
- Does his homework (2 points)
- Practices the piano (2 points)
- Sets the table (1 point)

Luke can use his points for:

- Watching TV for an additional thirty minutes (4 points)
- Playing video games for twenty minutes (4 points)
- Getting a special treat for dessert (4 points)
- Having Mom or Dad play a game with him (4 points)
- Staying up an extra twenty minutes at night (6 points)

- Having a friend over (8 points)
- Renting a video on the weekend (10 points)
- Going to the movies, museum, bowling, or miniature golfing on the weekend (20 points)

Building these lists may take trial, error, and negotiation. At first, many children like the system because they see it as a way of getting what they want. Other children get angry because they now have to *do* something to get what they previously would have gotten for nothing. For the incentive system to work, the child has to want to do it; he has to see that it can work to his benefit and that he is in control. The list of rewards has to be changed occasionally to retain the child's interest in the system, and parents must stick with the system even if everyone else appears to lose interest.

Once the incentive system is established as a way of rewarding compliance, it can also be used as a form of punishment. In other words, the child may begin to lose points or chips when he breaks rules.

TIME OUT Another method of managing noncompliance is "time out." Time out involves isolating the child in a "time-out chair" or corner of the room when he misbehaves. During time out, the child should have no access to any rewards, such as games or TV. Sending a child to his room—where he can play with toys—does not qualify as a time out. For young children, time outs can be kept short—two to five minutes. Time out should be imposed only for a few serious misbehaviors. For example, you might want to impose time out if your child hits someone or breaks something, but not if he calls someone a name. If time out is overused, it loses its effectiveness. For older children, time out is difficult to implement unless it has been done consistently since the child was small.

ADAPTING THE PROGRAM FOR YOUR CHILD The last few sessions of the parent-training class in Philadelphia help parents adapt the behavior-management program so that it addresses their own particular areas of difficulty. For example, some parents need help in developing coping strategies that can be applied in public places. Others need help in dealing with grandparents and extended family members. In addition, parents learn how to work more effectively with the child's particular school.

Learning effective behavior-management strategies for your ADHD child is hard work. It requires a long-term effort, vigilance, and persistence. You are likely to make mistakes along the way. You may be tempted to blame your child's current problems on ineffective management techniques that you used in the past. You may feel guilty about having to use techniques to "manipulate" your child. Parent-training classes can help you with these concerns because they give you an opportunity to discuss them. Many such programs include "booster" sessions that encourage you to keep up the hard work once your formal training is over.

Keep in mind that the majority of ADHD children's problems are not caused by ineffective parenting, and that ADHD children can put even the best parenting techniques to the test. But if you are able to make some headway in teaching your child better self-control and teaching him to get along more amicably with others (including you), you will give him a gift that will serve him well throughout his life.

BEHAVIOR THERAPY AT SCHOOL

Behavior-management strategies are often needed in the classroom as well as at home. Usually, parents do not have as much influence in the classroom as they do at home, and teachers rarely like to be told by parents how they should handle a child. A number of behavior-management techniques that have been used successfully in schools involve a home component as well. But even if the program you undertake does not require you to become involved at home, you will want to keep abreast of the program at school. It may influence your child's moods, tempers, and level of achievement in school, and you may be able to adapt some of the strategies for use at home.

School-based behavior-management programs should aim to teach children better means of self-control. Unfortunately, many are designed not as learning experiences for the child but as tools for the teacher to use to maintain order in the classroom. While such programs may satisfy the teacher's needs, they may not help your child grow and learn.

Behavior-management programs may be implemented by a teacher, guidance counselor, principal, school psychologist, or a private mental health professional. If the impetus for instituting the program comes from you or a professional you have hired rather than from the school itself, you are likely to have more input and become more involved. Here we discuss several types of school-based programs. They vary in their level of complexity and in the intensity of effort required to implement them. Some will be more acceptable to you than others, depending on your child's school, his teacher, and the structure of the classroom. If you are relying on the services of an outside psychologist, he will likely want to observe the classroom and consult with the teacher before he recommends a program. This will allow him to design a program that will work in the classroom setting and be acceptable to the teacher. He will also use this opportunity to try to enlist the teacher's support in implementing such a program.

THE DAILY REPORT A simple and low-intensive behavior-intervention program probably will involve "daily reports." These reports are cards that are filled out by the child's teachers and sent home to the parents. A daily report card lists behaviors such as "completed work," "stayed in seat," and "didn't bother others"; the teacher checks either yes or no for each behavior. Sometimes the parents dispense appropriate reinforcers at home; alternatively, rewards are given by the teacher in school. The daily reports can be adapted to a particular child's special areas of need. The parents and/or the psychologist set a goal that, if reached, allows the child to gain some reward at home. Generally, the goal that a child must reach in order to gain the reward should be kept low enough that the child will reach it on an average day. In order for a system like this to work, the child must feel he can succeed.

Daily report systems can be developed that target a few specific misbehaviors. For example, consider a little boy named Seth, whose class disruptions were creating problems.[10] His psychologist, in consultation with his teacher, identified four of Seth's most significant problem behaviors: getting out of his seat without permission, bothering other children in class, calling out, and disregarding directives from the teacher. The teacher set an allowable limit for each of these behaviors. She decided that initially she could put up with Seth getting out of his seat and calling out twice each day, but that she would tolerate only one infraction of the rule against bothering other children or disregarding her instructions.

The psychologist prepared daily report cards that sat on Seth's desk. One side of the cards tallied the behaviors that were problematic. The four behaviors were listed, and the teacher marked with a check each time Seth displayed that behavior. At the end of the day, the teacher added the check marks and gave Seth a "yes" on the other side of the card if he did not cross the day's limit for each behavior. The yesses were totaled at the end of the day; Seth received a reward from the teacher for each yes (see box).

A somewhat more complicated system was used with Alex. The psychologist identified four behaviors that Alex needed to control and the criteria for what constituted good behavior. He asked Alex's teachers to score Alex on his daily report as follows: 0 if he didn't meet the criteria that day, 1 if he did meet them, and 2 if he exceeded them (see box). Since Alex had five subjects each day, the teachers filled out one card for each subject. At the end of the day, Alex's points were totaled for all five subjects. The maximum number of

Behavior Tally

	Number of Times	Daily limit
1. Was out of seat without permission	_____	_____
2. Bothered others	_____	_____
3. Called out	_____	_____
4. Didn't mind teacher	_____	_____

Seth's Daily Report Card

TEACHER _____   CHILD _____

DATE _____

TIME PERIOD _____

	YES	NO
1. Completed work	_____	_____
2. Stayed in seat	_____	_____
3. Didn't bother others	_____	_____
4. Didn't call out	_____	_____
5. Minded teacher	_____	_____
6. Didn't argue with teacher during report	_____	_____
TOTAL	_____	_____

points that Alex could earn was 40. Depending on the number of points he earned at school, he was given poker chips at home that could be redeemed for various home-based rewards. At the beginning of the program, the psychologist recommended that Alex be able to earn rewards fairly easily, 80 to 90 percent of the time. The teachers filled out daily reports before the reward system started to help determine

Alex's "baseline," 8 points. In other words, Alex was usually able to earn at least 8 points, for which he would get one chip. If he received 10 to 12 points, he got two chips; 14 to 16 points, three chips, and so on. Alex and his parents drew up a list of rewards from which he could choose for the chips he earned. For one chip, he could play video games for twenty minutes or watch TV. For two chips, he could have a friend over or work on a project with his father for twenty minutes. Alex could save up his chips for a bigger reward on the weekend, but had to use at least one chip a day on a daily reward. Weekend rewards included things like going to the movies or spending the day with his grandmother. Alex's teachers were not told what his baseline was; they were asked only to issue the points. This was done so that the teachers were not subjectively determining whether Alex would get a reward; instead, he was able to control the rewards through his behavior.

When the program started, Alex earned 8 to 9 points on most days, but he quickly realized how easily he could do better. Within a few weeks he was regularly earning 20 to 25 points. He liked the daily report system because it allowed him to have some control over special activities. His teachers liked the system because his behavior in class improved dramatically with minimal effort on their part. His parents liked it because they now knew on a day-to-day basis what was happening at school. The system had other benefits as well. Alex frequently chose rewards that involved special projects with his mother or father, and this improved the relationship between Alex and his parents.

Over time, the point system was adjusted to reflect Alex's new baseline, and the list of rewards changed in order to maintain Alex's interest in the program. Alex's parents, teachers, and psychologist stayed in contact to reevaluate the program at frequent intervals and to make adjustments as needed.

Alex's Daily Report

Instructions: Please rate each behavior using a point system from
the following scale:

   0   did not meet criteria
   1   did meet criteria
   2   exceeded criteria

Child's name: _____ Date: _____

Behavior   Rating

1. completed homework   _____

2. completed seatwork   _____

3. listened to instructions   _____

4. cooperated with classroom rules regarding
    conduct   _____

                          Total   _____

CONTINGENCY MANAGEMENT AND RESPONSE COST Daily report
systems offer the advantage that they are relatively easy to
implement and do not require much special effort on the
teacher's part. But for many children, a daily report system
will not be enough. One drawback is that the reward it offers
for a positive behavior is somewhat delayed. When the response to a behavior is immediate, children are usually more
likely to modify their behavior. Another drawback of daily
report systems is that they offer only positive reinforcers. Approaches that use only positive reinforcers can be effective,
but approaches that apply negative consequences for inappropriate behaviors, in addition to rewards for appropriate behaviors, have been shown in several studies to be more effective.

Other behavior-management approaches do offer immediate consequences, both positive and negative. Behavior-management techniques that require children to fulfill certain criteria before they receive a benefit are called *contingency management techniques.* For example, one contingency management technique is to set up a morning routine for the child that requires him to get up on his own, get dressed, make his bed, and brush his teeth *before* he can come downstairs for breakfast. Receiving breakfast is made contingent on his completing the other requirements. The reward—breakfast—is immediate and salient.

Contingency management systems that deliver immediate negative consequences for inappropriate behaviors may also be devised. One such technique, called *response cost,* involves taking away points or privileges whenever a child misbehaves. For example, a child might be told that at the end of the school day, he will have a twenty-minute free play period, but that for every rule infraction he will lose one minute. This child might have a set of twenty flip cards on the corner of his desk. Each time the teacher observes an inappropriate behavior, she flips a card over. The child sees immediately the negative consequence of his action—that is, he sees his free time dwindling away.

Response cost is more punitive than a daily report or contingency management system, but it has the advantage of being more salient and thus may be easier for a child with attention deficits to follow. It can be used in conjunction with a positive reward system. For example, a child might be able to earn points for appropriate behaviors, such as paying attention, bringing in homework, and completing assignments on time; or he may lose points for inappropriate behaviors, such as not paying attention, talking during quiet times, and getting up from his seat. These points could be exchanged throughout the day for favored activities or items. When a child's inappropriate behavior involves an inability to stay focused on a given task, the system can be designed so that at predetermined times—for instance, every five minutes—the teacher checks to see whether the child is on task and deducts points if he is not. Again, she lets the child know immediately if he has lost points.

Contingency management and response-cost systems require more teacher participation and thus may be unacceptable to teachers who feel that they cannot devote much extra attention to one particular child. When used appropriately, however, these techniques can be quite powerful.

SOCIAL-SKILLS TRAINING

Another kind of behavior therapy that is sometimes recommended for ADHD children is social-skills training. Many children with ADHD have trouble getting along in social situations. Their short fuses and inattentive, impulsive behaviors, combined with their low self-esteem, make them bossy, aggressive, and disruptive around their peers. Moreover, they often have trouble picking up on and interpreting nonverbal social cues from other children. Social-skills training attempts to teach such children better ways of interacting, solving problems, cooperating, and communicating. In small groups, the children are taught through instruction, modeling, and role-playing how to deal more effectively with difficult situations that may arise. The children then try out their skills in play settings set up within the small groups.

In theory, social-skills training appears to be a useful addition to other forms of behavior therapy, but its effectiveness with ADHD children has not been supported by several studies. Children may learn social skills that they can apply in an artificial group setting, but they may find it difficult to use the skills in their real world. In other words, the skills do not appear to "generalize." In addition, problems with peer relationships are often very resistant to change and require long-term interventions that may be impractical in a group therapy setting. Social-skills training that is incorporated into the regular school curriculum may be more effective since it occurs in a more naturalistic setting and can be reinforced year after year. In addition social-skills programs set up within school can take advantage of the natural reinforcers in a child's world. For example, children may covet the role of "team captain" in a certain school game; this might be a desirable reward for a child who displays appropriate social behavior.

School-based social-skills programs involve training teachers and playground aides to cue and reward positive social (prosocial) behaviors in children, such as listening when someone else is talking, taking turns, sharing, and making a new friend. Psychologist Thomas J. Power of the ADHD Clinic has implemented a novel program in a nearby school. His program includes establishing a "prosocial behavior of the week," in which everyone in the school—teachers, children, aides, and parents—all work on one specific prosocial behavior each week. Programs such as this one benefit all children in the school, not just those who have weaker social skills.

COGNITIVE THERAPY

Cognitive therapy aims to teach children problem-solving strategies and skills that they can apply in the classroom and in social situations. It teaches them self-control over their impulsive and inattentive behaviors and to "stop, look, and listen" before responding. Cognitive therapy uses games, role playing, self-instruction, and other problem-solving approaches to teach children specific strategies.

Cognitive therapy has been used quite successfully to treat adults with depression, anxiety, and panic disorders, but for children with ADHD, it has been less successful. Though many children can learn to control their behavior during therapy sessions, they have trouble applying the skills consistently in school and maintaining those skills over a long period of time. This may be because their behavioral problems arise from inborn biological and temperamental characteristics more than from a lack of particular skills or from not understanding how to behave appropriately. Thus, their inattentiveness and impulsivity may need to be controlled medically before cognitive training can be successful. For this reason, some therapists use cognitive-therapy techniques as an adjunct to other forms of medical and behavioral treatment, reasoning that while cognitive therapy does not affect the core symptoms of ADHD to any significant extent, it may add to the child's repertoire of appropriate skills.

Cognitive approaches are increasingly used in combination with behavioral methods, resulting in what are called *cognitive-behavioral methods.* Such methods can train children to self-monitor their behavior, with a supervising adult available to verify the accuracy of their ratings and to provide reinforcement. This teaches children to manage their own difficulties and to develop their own compensatory strategies.

Cognitive-behavioral methods were used with ten-year-old Tina, who was bright but very impulsive and tended to act in an arrogant manner. Tina did not respond to Ritalin and developed side effects with other kinds of medication. Behavioral approaches were used, but they had minimal effects. Finally, Tina's psychologist implemented a self-monitoring program that required Tina to rate her own behavior. Her task was to try to match her self-ratings with those of her teacher. This approach forced her to pay more attention to her own behavior, and thus she learned that she could control herself.

WORKING WITH YOUR CHILD'S TEACHERS

In order for any behavioral intervention to be successful, parents and teachers must coordinate their efforts. But sometimes parent-teacher cooperation is difficult to establish. Teachers may feel that they have already tried to accommodate the child's difficulties and that nothing has worked. They may resent the psychologist who comes in to observe their teaching methods, feeling that they are on trial or are being blamed for the child's troubles. They may not appreciate outside interference from the child's doctor, psychologist, or parent. For their part, parents may feel frustrated by what they perceive as a lack of accommodation from the child's teachers. They may feel that the teachers focus too intently on the child's weaknesses and don't give him credit for his abilities. Some parents feel locked in battle with teachers who are unwilling to cooperate.

When the parent-teacher relationship erodes to the point that each views the other as part of the problem rather than as part of the solution, intervention by a psychologist or behavior specialist may relieve some of the hostility. Many parent-teacher relationships improve naturally once the child begins to respond to behavior-management strategies imposed by the therapist. When parent-teacher hostilities are more severe, a therapist may temporarily act as a buffer between them, working with each separately to help the child function better. In time, the therapist tries to facilitate a better working relationship between the parents and teachers.

Some relaxation of hostilities may be brought about through education. Teachers who have a clearer understanding of the nature of ADHD may be more willing to accept suggestions regarding management. Psychologists may help smooth over difficulties through understanding, since they are in a position to appreciate the difficulties and frustrations encountered by both the teacher and the parents. Their viewpoint may help each side to understand the problems of the other.

Parents can help promote cooperation with the school by taking a constructive and positive attitude with teachers. Appreciate the fact that each day the teacher faces a class full of children with different needs and expectations and that she may lack the support services necessary to give your child what he needs. She may be unaware of small changes that can be made in the classroom to alleviate some of your child's difficulties. Finally, she may feel unappreciated for the efforts she has already made.

When you begin a behavior-therapy program, let the teacher know that you appreciate the extra effort she is willing to make. Try to maintain frequent contact with the teacher without making added demands. Most teachers appreciate parents who show genuine concern for their child's classroom behavior and performance. Ask the teacher to contact you if she has problems with the new system. Thank her for any special efforts she makes; send notes of appreciation when appropriate; offer to go along on class trips or help with classroom projects. Any effort you make to reach out to the teacher in a positive way will likely prove beneficial.

You or the psychologist may also wish to seek help from a guidance counselor, school psychologist, or principal. Such a person can be particularly helpful if your child has more than one teacher. Many children benefit from having one key person with whom they interact on a daily basis. If you are really lucky, you may find someone in the school who is willing to take your child on as a "project." If this person is someone other than a classroom teacher, she may be able to help ease your child's transition from one grade to the next.

Despite your best efforts, you may continue to feel frustrated by the services available for your child or by what you perceive as a lack of willingness on the part of the school or teachers to make accommodations for your child. In addition, you may feel that the school is recommending or demanding interventions that are not appropriate. In the next chapter, we discuss different educational options that you may want to consider.

CHAPTER 8

Educational Placement

Though ADHD can create difficulties in many aspects of children's lives, school usually presents the biggest challenge. Not only does school occupy a major part of children's time, it is usually not structured for children with the temperamental characteristics of ADHD. School programs are not designed for children who have trouble sitting still or paying attention. School underachievement and misbehavior are the most frequent characteristics that lead to the assessment, diagnosis, and treatment of ADHD. Yet surprisingly, schools were not a major focus of intervention for ADHD until recently. Instead of trying to modify school programs in order to achieve a better fit with the children, most doctors, teachers, and parents focused on modifying the children pharmacologically to make them fit into the school as it is.

But the medical focus of ADHD treatment is now shifting. The American Academy of Pediatrics recently issued a statement that medication should not be used alone in the treatment of ADHD; rather, "proper classroom placement, physical education programs, behavior modifications, counseling, and provision of structure" should be tried *first*. Still, despite this increased emphasis on school-based interventions, many schools do not offer any services designed to meet the special needs of children with ADHD.

At the ADHD Clinic at The Children's Hospital of Philadelphia and its associates, a major emphasis is placed on identifying appropriate school-based interventions. This may mean finding a better class placement or implementing structural modifications in the existing classroom. It is often a long process, as schools are responding slowly to their increasing responsibilities.

As a parent, you may feel frustrated in your search for an appropriate school placement for your ADHD child. In this chapter, we discuss some of the options available for children with ADHD and some of the steps you can take to be sure that your child receives an appropriate education. Educational programs vary significantly from state to state and from locality to locality, so your options may be limited. But if you know what to look for, you are more likely to find a suitable program or help shape a program that meets your child's needs. We also discuss your child's legal rights to appropriate educational services.

OPTIMIZING THE SCHOOL ENVIRONMENT

Many children with ADHD can function adequately in regular classrooms, but they do not function optimally there. Certain types of teachers and classrooms are better able than others to meet ADHD children's academic, social, and emotional needs. The ideal teacher for such children is highly skilled in both teaching strategies and behavior-management techniques; she is well organized and establishes clear rules with consistent, firm limits. At the same time, she makes learning fun. Beyond these qualities, she is willing to take your child on as a "project." She sees him as a challenge, not as a problem, and she sees him as an individual, not as an "ADHD child." She is willing to collaborate with you, consult with outside experts, and try novel approaches. She is well supported by the school administration and faculty.

The ideal classroom is relatively small, with classroom aides available to assist with behavior-management programs and social-skills training exercises. Behavioral specialists are available to work with the teachers and to teach social skills as part of the curriculum. Reading and math specialists are available for remedial help if necessary. The curriculum is flexible both in content and in workload so that it can be adjusted to fit with children's abilities and needs. Since unstructured classrooms are frequently overly distracting to children with ADHD, structured flexibility is optimal.

Where do you find this ideal teacher and the ideal classroom? Most parents do not choose either the school their child attends or the teachers he has. Still, within most school systems there are some avenues that parents can explore to find the best situation for their child. If the school offers more than one teacher at each grade level, you may be able to observe or speak with the different teachers in order to find the one who is most adaptable to your child's needs. Some schools do not allow parents to request specific teachers, but you may have the opportunity to give some input in the selection process. Perhaps you can arrange a meeting with the principal to discuss your child's specific needs and the type of classroom that would be best for him. Or perhaps you can ask your child's current teacher to recommend or request a specific teacher for next year. If your school has guidance counselors or school psychologists, you could enlist their support in finding the appropriate placement for your child. Or, if a psychologist or behavior therapist is treating your child, you might ask him to contact the school and make some recommendations regarding your child's placement. As much as possible, try to work within the system and try not to antagonize school officials or teachers; but at the same time, advocate for your child to be sure his needs are being met.

In frustration with schools' regular offerings, some parents try to have their child placed in special classes for learning-disabled (LD) children or socially and emotionally disturbed (SED) children. But such a placement is not always appropriate for ADHD children. To be sure, some children with ADHD are also learning disabled or have relatively severe behavioral problems. Such children do benefit from these special classes. But most ADHD children do not meet the criteria for these classes, even when they have learning difficulties or behavioral problems. Thus, these classes do not meet the academic, social, and emotional needs of most ADHD children. Special classes may even stigmatize children further and lead them to internalize a sense of being different or abnormal.

Such was the case with Melissa, a six-year-old girl with UADD (undifferentiated ADD, or ADD without hyperactivity). Melissa's psychological testing suggested that she had an auditory processing deficit. But she did not qualify for special education because her achievement test scores and her performance at school indicated that she was only six months to one year below her grade level. Her psychologist felt that a special education class would be too stigmatizing for her. He recommended that she stay in the regular classroom and that she get extra help from the reading specialist and social-skills training. Further, he suggested that her parents discuss a medication trial with her pediatrician.

Situations such as Melissa's leave parents in a quandary. Neither the regular classes nor the special classes are set up for children with ADHD, so what is the right educational placement for them? The answer to this question may come in the next few years, as the federal and state governments, prodded by parent and professional groups, address the problem of educating ADHD children. Federal law already states that all children are entitled to a free and appropriate education. How that law applies to children with ADHD has yet to be determined.

A Free and Appropriate Education

Public Law 94-142, originally passed in 1975, obligates states to provide a free and appropriate education to all children, regardless of their handicaps. The law recognizes a number of specific handicaps, including "serious emotional disturbances" and "specific learning disabilities." Serious emotional disturbances include psychiatric conditions such as schizophrenia and depression, but not behavior disorders such as ADHD. Specific learning disabilities are disorders that result in problems with spoken- or written-language processing and that affect a child's ability to listen, think, speak, read, write, spell, or do mathematical calculations.

According to the letter of the law, only a small proportion of children with ADHD qualify for services under PL 94-142. The reality is, however, that a large number of children in LD classes around the country do not have language-processing deficits but do have learning difficulties related to ADHD. They are enrolled in LD classes because many school districts apply the term *learning disabled* to any child whose achievement lags two years or more behind his grade level. Unfortunately, children who are in LD classes because their ADHD has affected their ability to learn may not be receiving educational services appropriate to their areas of difficulty.

ADHD children in LD classes account for only about one-fourth to one-third of all ADHD children. Most children with ADHD remain in regular classrooms without any special education help. There they usually experience learning difficulties as well as negative social and emotional consequences. In other words, children with ADHD frequently slip through the cracks; they fit neither in the regular classroom nor in special LD or SED classes.

The solution to this problem may ultimately take the form of amendments to PL 94-142 that would specify ADHD as a handicapping condition and require that appropriate educational programs be provided for ADHD children. Such programs would likely place children in mainstream classrooms rather than in pull-out programs. Some parent and professional groups are currently lobbying for such changes in the law, but they meet with resistance from those who argue that ADHD does not exist.

Other parents use another federal law, the Rehabilitation

Act of 1973, to obtain services for their children. Section 504 of this act prohibits federally financed programs, including schools, from discriminating against anyone because of a handicap. In at least two cases in which children with ADHD were denied special services, the courts ruled that ADHD constitutes a handicapping condition and that schools are obligated under Section 504 to provide appropriate education to them.

Whether PL 94-142 or Section 504 is ultimately used to provide appropriate educational programming for children with ADHD, it seems likely that schools in the future will have to take responsibility in some way. What form this special programming will take is not yet clear, but it will probably include better screening procedures, teacher training, training of paraprofessionals such as playground aides and bus drivers, and regular classroom interventions. According to many ADHD experts, most ADHD children would best be served by enrolling in regular classrooms but with specific behavioral interventions. Many such interventions can be implemented without major disruptions to the existing classroom structure. Even before changes in the law are made, some schools are willing to accommodate the special needs of children with ADHD.

School Interventions

Behavior-management systems such as those discussed in chapter 7 would be the major type of school-based intervention. Such strategies could be used to modify the behaviors that present the most difficulty for children with ADHD: following directions, getting started, staying on task for the required length of time, working independently when necessary, keeping quiet and still when necessary, getting along with teachers and peers, and switching smoothly from one activity to another. Contingency management systems using rewards and mild negative consequences could be established to shape these appropriate behaviors.

Beyond these behavior-modification programs, teachers can be trained to make minor modifications in their teaching methods that will work better with ADHD children. For example, many children with ADHD have trouble following directions. A teacher might cue such children that she is going to give directions before she actually does so by touching their shoulders. She could try to establish eye contact with the children, simplify and shorten instructions, and check periodically to make sure they understand.

Both behavior-modification programs and modified teaching methods require extensive teacher training if they are to be effective. Currently, most teachers receive little formalized training in teaching students with ADHD. In-service programs or other courses could rectify this deficiency by teaching teachers about the characteristics of ADHD and about the educational, social, and emotional needs of children with ADHD. Teachers must learn to adjust their expectations of children with ADHD and to work within the children's particular capabilities. For example, some children with ADHD have organizational deficits and need assistance in maintaining order in their desks, notebooks, and bookbags. Sometimes teachers will have to accommodate children with such problems, such as by giving them pencils when they can't find one in their desks rather than punishing them for forgetting their pencils.

An appropriate educational program for children with ADHD would also include social-skills training as part of the curriculum (see chapter 7). In the best of circumstances, social-skills training would be extended to areas outside of the classroom, to the playground, cafeteria, and school bus. These parts of the school day often present the most serious difficulties for children with ADHD. In many schools, they are relatively unstructured times, and adults intervene only when activities get out of hand. But research has suggested that introducing some structure into those time periods can prevent aggressive and antisocial activities from becoming troublesome.

Children with ADHD enrolled in regular classrooms may need additional tutoring or remedial help to keep pace with or catch up to the rest of the class. If your child is experiencing academic difficulty, check into the remedial services available in his school, such as a reading specialist or resource room. If the school does not have an established program for remedial help, you may wish to arrange for private tutoring.

In some parts of the country, public schools already offer programs that can be adapted to meet the needs of ADHD children. In addition, some parents are in a position to choose alternatives to the public schools. If you are considering sending your child to a private school, you should investigate not only the resources available at the school but also the academic and social demands that would be placed on your child there. Avoid a school that would be inflexible either in its educational approach or in its academic demands. A good school for a child with ADHD would individualize the educational approach for each child, offer a social-skills program to deal with problems in the context of the regular day, and employ a behavioral consultant when necessary. In such a school, teachers work with support teams of other teachers to define the best approach for particular children.

The demands the school places on students may also influence the treatment course your child will need. In a school that emphasizes one-to-one interaction between teacher and student, an ADHD child may be able to function quite well without medication, but in a different school situation he might need medication. In a school that places heavy academic demands on its students, a child who might not ordinarily need medication may flounder without it.

This was a major consideration when Matthew's parents were considering whether to send him to the public school in their neighborhood or to a private school. The private school was more academically demanding, which they felt would be an advantage for Matthew, who was a superior student. But the private school's demands were so great that their pediatrician recommended stimulant medication if they chose it. At the public school, he said, medication would probably not be necessary. After much soul-searching and weighing of the risks and benefits associated with both choices, Matthew's parents chose the private school and medication. They reasoned that the more demanding environment would allow him to gain significant benefits both academically and in terms of self-esteem.

Generally, children with moderate to severe ADHD need medication regardless of their school environment. But the needs of children with mild ADHD depends on the skill level of the parents, the organization of the family, the resources within the school, and the motivation of the teachers.

As the parent of a child with ADHD, you must try to determine what educational environment will best meet your child's needs, as well as the needs and resources of your family. You may have to actively advocate for your child; parent advocacy is discussed in chapter 13.

CHAPTER 9

Family Therapy

When a child has ADHD, his whole family is affected. Not only do the child's difficulties add stress to the family, but the family is usually involved in the diagnostic process and in the design and execution of management strategies. In earlier chapters we have discussed the primary management approaches: medication, behavior management, and educational placement. For any of these approaches to be successful, family participation is essential. But sometimes family conflicts get in the way of effective intervention. When this is the case, the families may benefit from outside counseling or therapy.

In this chapter, we discuss issues that can interfere with a family's ability to raise and nurture their child with ADHD. You may recognize some of these problems in your own family. If you feel that you need assistance in exploring these issues further, you may want to seek the services of a counselor or therapist. Unfortunately, there is no clear-cut method for determining whether further counseling is indicated or what type of counseling best suits your needs.

Sometimes family counseling may be incorporated into other aspects of treatment and management. Parent training often involves considerable discussion about family conflicts and how they affect your ability to apply what you have learned. Consulting a psychologist or counselor about behavior-management techniques may mean discussing family difficulties as they present themselves. For many families, such low-intensive family-counseling intervention is sufficient. But when family conflicts persist or are extremely severe, more intense family therapy may be valuable.

Moreover, when issues arise that seem difficult to resolve, other types of therapy may be indicated. A parent who is seriously depressed may benefit from psychological counseling; parents between whom conflict has escalated to a point that they find it difficult to work together may find that marital therapy helps.

WHERE TO TURN

Family counseling may be obtained in a number of ways. Many psychologists, psychiatrists, and social workers provide counseling and therapy services for entire families. Some of these professionals call themselves family therapists or family counselors, while others call themselves psychologists, psychiatrists, or behavior therapists. These titles actually tell you little about a therapist's approach. Even professionals who call themselves family therapists use a wide variety of therapeutic approaches. Some are insight oriented—that is, they try to uncover underlying emotions and hidden feelings—while others attack behaviors directly. Behaviorally oriented counselors themselves use different strategies. Some emphasize making modifications in a child's environment, including the school, more than others do. Many family therapists incorporate both insight-oriented and behavioral approaches. Generally, psychiatrists deal with more severe problems than psychologists do. A psychiatrist is appropriate if one or more family members requires a medication besides Ritalin, which may be prescribed by your family doctor or pediatrician in consultation with a behavior therapist. Psychologists and social workers tend to do more instructing and teaching than psychiatrists do, although some psychiatrists incorporate parent training into their family work.

If you decide to seek family counseling, you should look for a therapist who is knowledgeable about ADHD. Usually this means a therapist with a strong behavioral orientation. To find a counselor who suits your needs, you may want to ask for a referral from your family physician or pediatrician or other health-care professional who is working with your child on ADHD-related issues. Other possible referral sources include ADHD parent support or advocacy groups (see appendix), ADHD clinics in large medical centers, family social-service agencies, and other parents of children with ADHD or similar behavioral difficulties.

Keep in mind that psychotherapy and counseling are not themselves treatments for ADHD. Rather, they are avenues by which you may be able to improve the overall climate of your family relationships and change negative interactions into positive ones. In the long run, this should help both your child with ADHD as well as the rest of the family. But counseling is no substitute for other forms of treatment.

PROMOTING HEALTHFUL FAMILY INTERACTIONS

The approach that your therapist takes in helping your family depends to a great extent on the nature of your family's difficulties. In some families, one or both parents are unwilling to accept that their child actually has a problem. Sometimes parents are so angry with each other that they have difficulty working together to help their child. Other families are in disarray because the parents do not see eye-to-eye on how to best manage their ADHD child's difficulties. Though different therapists approach families in different ways, family work usually concentrates on three common themes: regaining control, accepting the diagnosis and implications of ADHD, and confronting anger.

REGAINING CONTROL Parents of children with ADHD often feel that despite all their hard work, they have no control over their children's actions. They feel beaten down and defeated. They get angry, and the child gets angry in reaction to the parents' anger. The parents become enraged, and the child gets enraged in turn. The cycle of defeat repeats itself over and over and begins again when the child acts up. To break this cycle and regain control, parents must first understand how they are drawn into the cycle and how it leads them to lose hope and control. They must learn how to regain control not only over their child but over their own emotions in this volatile situation.

In order to reestablish control, parents must first look at how their parenting styles may be contributing to the difficulties. Parents who are inconsistent, unsure of themselves, competitive with each other, working at cross-purposes, or incapacitated by their anger at each other will be unable to regain control over their children. Such problems can occur in any family, but ADHD children's difficulties often exacerbate conflicts between parents. At the same time, children with ADHD tend to have difficulty with self-control and thus are in special need of guidance from their parents.

Inconsistency between parents is probably the most common cause of ineffective parenting. Some fathers rely on toughness, while mothers are more likely to try pleading with or encouraging the child. The mother may give the child one instruction during the day, while the father says something contradictory when he comes home from work, unaware of the earlier instruction from the mother. One parent may be very angry with the child, while the other parent tries to protect the child from that anger. Whenever there is parental inconsistency, children are likely to become confused by the mixed messages they are receiving. They recognize the loopholes created by the parents' lack of agreement and may play one parent off the other. The parents may argue about whose parenting style is more effective, thereby increasing the conflict. Such conflict eats away at the marriage and at the parents' feeling of control over the situation.

In order to alleviate such conflicts, parents must explore

their parenting styles, identify their inconsistencies, and develop a mutually agreeable plan of action. A therapist can guide parents through this process and help them avoid becoming sidetracked by blaming each other for the difficulties. If this exploration uncovers other sources of conflict between the parents or other parent-child conflicts, the therapist can guide the family to explore those issues.

Michael

Michael was an angry and frustrated child with angry and frustrated parents. They had tried numerous times to rein in his oppositional behavior, but they did so in a rather haphazard way. They had difficulty establishing clear limits for Michael in part because they could not agree on what those limits should be. As the family conflicts mounted, their marriage deteriorated, increasing the anxiety and tension in Michael and his brother. Finally, they sought family therapy. The therapist began by setting up a behavior-management plan for Michael. Because it was designed by a third party, Michael's parents found it easy to adhere to without becoming sidetracked by their anger at each other. The therapist also helped them see how important it was that they react consistently and support each other. Within several weeks, they began to see dramatic improvements in Michael's behavior, and the therapist was able to deal with other aspects of the family's anger and frustration.

Another factor that weakens parents' sense of control is *confusion* about the child's capabilities. It can be difficult to know whether an ADHD child is really incapable of controlling his own impulses or whether he is using his disability as an excuse for obnoxious behavior. Some parents blame the child for his inconsistencies and inabilities, while others are overprotective and excuse the child's every weakness, attributing his failures to "his problem." Neither of these positions helps the child master his difficulties effectively. Both the parents and the child need to learn all they can about ADHD and about the child's particular difficulties, so that they can establish realistic expectations and goals.

Sometimes, *competition* between parents about different parenting styles creates so much conflict that the child begins to blame himself for their troubles. When this happens, parents must identify the source of their anger and frustration and understand that the child may be the trigger without being the cause of their blow-ups. A therapist can help the parents see how their conflicts are being misinterpreted by the child. At the same time, the therapist can work with the child to help him see that he is not to blame.

Some parents are unable to exert control over the children out of *fear*. When parents are afraid of their child, the control issues cannot be tackled until the parents' fear is conquered. Occasionally, an extremely aggressive or destructive child requires hospitalization so that his conduct can be brought under control and the parents can begin to work on their fears in a tightly controlled situation.

Understanding why the parents have given up control tackles only half the problem. Parents must also learn techniques for *exerting and maintaining control.* Parent training and other behavior-management approaches can serve this function (see chapter 7). When parent training is incorporated into family counseling, parents may have the opportunity to try out certain techniques in the presence of the therapist, who can offer support and encouragement during the process.

Sometimes parents' methods of control must be unlearned, such as beating a child for misbehavior. Beating may achieve the goal of getting the child to do what is asked of him, but it teaches him to become a bully at the same time. Further, parents who beat their children lose their moral edge and the respect of their children.

When parents regain control of their child, it benefits the whole family. Parental self-esteem goes up as they regain a sense of mastery and competence. In addition, the child is reassured because his lack of self-control can be extremely

Tim

The first time five-year-old Tim and his family came in for therapy, Tim tore up the room within five minutes while his parents were talking with the therapist. Tim's parents said that at home they used a time-out system to deal with such behavior, but that the system rarely worked. So the therapist told them to go ahead and make it work there, in the office. For twenty minutes, the parents demanded that Tim sit in the time-out chair for one minute until he calmed. Tim screamed, bit, and threw things. The therapist encouraged the parents to remain calm and stick with it. When Tim finally sat still for one minute, the parents said it was the first time in years that they had gotten him to obey. It had required a lot of work and persistence on their part, but it proved to them that they could do it if they worked together and didn't give up. That was a turning point in their management of Tim's behavior. The parents finally knew that they were in control, and Tim knew that he could not beat them down. The next time he threw a temper tantrum, it took only three minutes to get him to sit in the time-out chair.

scary to him. Many ADHD children know that they cannot bring themselves under control and that they need extra help from their parents.

Sometimes parents are blocked from assuming control by their own feelings of inadequacy, guilt, anger, or isolation. All these feelings are part of the normal process of coming to terms with the diagnosis of ADHD. But when they begin to get in the way of effective parenting, a family counselor may be able to help.

ACCEPTING THE DIAGNOSIS AND IMPLICATIONS OF ADHD Acceptance of the ADHD diagnosis comes more easily to some parents than to others. Some go through a grieving process as they see their hopes and expectations for their child dashed. For example, in the introduction you met Danny and his parents, who learned that he had ADHD when Danny was four. Danny's mother said she felt "devastated" when she first learned of the diagnosis. She had expected the psychiatrist to say that her son, who was extremely bright, misbehaved simply out of boredom. But instead, Danny's mother had to come to grips with the idea that her brilliant, beautiful son suffered from "a disorder." Over time, Danny's mother learned that the ADHD diagnosis was more a description of her son's difficulties than a prescription for an unhappy life. But that point of acceptance did not come either easily or quickly.

Parents grieve over the ADHD diagnosis in different ways. Some grieve openly from the beginning. Others become angry with the child or with themselves, with their parents, the school, or the doctor who delivered the diagnosis. Some deny the diagnosis altogether and search for other explanations of the child's difficulties. Still others accept the diagnosis immediately and begin to devise coping strategies. There is no "right" way to grieve. What works for one person may not work for you. But it is important to acknowledge whatever feelings you are experiencing; if you do not, they may come back to you in insidious ways. The parent who feels sad but holds those feelings inside may become depressed. The parent who doesn't express his anger may act out those feelings in an indirect but destructive way.

Educating yourself about ADHD can help relieve some of the guilt, anger, and anxiety you may feel. As you learn more about ADHD, you may begin to understand that neither you nor your child is to blame for the conflicts. Your feelings of hopelessness may be replaced by hope as you identify strategies that are likely to be effective with your child. You will learn that you are not alone. Other parents—probably some whom you know—are facing many of the same difficulties, with similar self-doubts and sad feelings. You may be able to link up with some of these parents, which will reduce your feelings of isolation. This can go a long way toward improving your effectiveness as a parent.

Children with ADHD also need to learn to accept their disability. They need to learn that the diagnosis doesn't mean that they are bad or stupid. Some children's inner sense of self-worth is badly damaged by school failures, lack of understanding, and criticism. Counseling can help such children rebuild a stronger and more positive vision of themselves. In chapter 11 we discuss some of the social and emotional issues that children with ADHD face.

CONFRONTING ANGER In families affected by ADHD, anger frequently simmers. ADHD children may be angry because they feel constantly picked on or because they are not given credit for their efforts. Siblings may be angry because so much attention is focused on their brother or sister. The mother may be angry at the father because she feels she bears more of the burden of caring for their difficult child. The father may be angry at the mother for not doing a better job. The possible sources of anger are too numerous to list, but the first step in confronting anger is to identify them. Who is angry about what? What are the things that cause resentment?

Anger can be particularly troublesome for parents who have difficulty controlling their own tempers or who have a low frustration tolerance. Anger can be fueled further when parents have not truly accepted their child's disability, when they have not grieved adequately, or when they themselves have low self-esteem. Finally, anger can build up when parents feel guilty about their angry feelings and thus refuse to express their frustrations.

Family therapy may be able to help families blocked by unresolved anger. It can serve as a safe place for all family members to talk about their anger. It may offer family members an opportunity to try out different ways of dealing with their anger. When anger starts to build during a therapy session, the family therapist may help guide the family through a successful resolution of the problem. For example, if the child throws a temper tantrum during the session, the family therapist can help the parents to stay calm and manage the tantrum without becoming enraged. Sometimes the therapist must teach the parents alternative means of behavior control, such as time out or restraint. After the situation has been brought under control, the therapist can guide the family through a discussion of the anger points so that they better understand the cycle of anger they are trying to avoid.

Anger between the husband and wife frequently flares in ADHD families. Different parenting styles can become major sources of conflict. In addition, the demands ADHD children place on parents can be intense. Frequently, one parent —usually the mother—shoulders more of the burden. As a result, she may be carrying years of built-up frustration and anger at both the child and her husband. When anger begins to build during a therapy session, the therapist might stop the action and ask the parents to describe what might happen next. Then they might look at alternatives to letting the argument escalate into a major battle. Sometimes anger between the parents is so intense that marital and/or individual therapy is required in addition to family therapy.

PAST HISTORY REVISITED The difficulties that some families experience may be influenced by past history. For example, a difficult child may remind a parent of someone else with whom there is unresolved anger. When this happens, the parent's reaction to the child is fueled not by the child's behavior but by his own unresolved emotional issues. In situations such as this, the parent's reactions to the child may seem out of proportion to the child's behavior. The parent may feel victimized by the child or enraged by seemingly minor infractions. The family therapist will want to find out what situations in the parent's past history led him to feel victimized, and who else elicited such rage. When the parent begins to understand that he is transferring his own unresolved anger at another person onto his child, he may be able to resolve that anger and move on to more appropriate reactions to his child.

Past history may also come into play when parents transfer family myths or family cultural assumptions onto the child. A mother who says "He's just like his father" or "He's just like my brother was" may be making assumptions about the child that do not apply. If the child's father or the mother's brother was disliked or frequently got into trouble, she may be assuming that the child will also have those attributes. Meanwhile, the father or brother may feel protective of the child, which can set up a collusion between the child and the father or brother that puts them at odds with the mother.

FAMILIES WITH SPECIAL NEEDS

Sometimes family interactions are complicated by special situations. Two such situations are of particular interest to ADHD-affected families. One is the family in which one parent has ADHD, and the other is the family in which the parents have separated or divorced.

When a parent has ADHD, effective parenting can be blocked by still further problems. Some parents feel relieved to learn that the trouble they have experienced throughout their lives has a name and an explanation. But at the same time, they may feel angry about the years during which they had to deal with repeated failure, lack of understanding, and diminished self-esteem (see chapter 12). Some parents feel guilty about passing the disorder on to their children; others refuse to accept their own diagnosis altogether. A parent's reaction to his own diagnosis can dramatically influence his effectiveness as a parent. The affected parent sometimes identifies so closely with the child's difficulties that he finds it difficult to act with authority; at the same time, he is trying to deal with his own conflicting emotions.

Another aspect to consider when one parent has ADHD is the response of the other parent. Usually, the parent with ADHD is the father, and the ADHD child is a son. If the father overidentifies with the son's difficulties, he may be quick to excuse misbehavior, leaving the mother feeling unsupported. On top of that, the mother may be angry with both the father and the son for constantly messing up and for having to keep after them to stay organized.

This was one of the problems festering in Michael's family, whom we met earlier in this chapter. Both Michael and his father were very disorganized, and his mother felt overburdened by their needs. In a case like theirs, counseling can help a father learn to accept and cope with his difficulties; it can help a mother better understand the father's difficulties and adopt a more constructive approach to both her husband and her son. And it can help both parents resolve their angry feelings. Part of Michael's family's work involved dealing with each person's anger and frustration and finding ways of renegotiating family responsibilities.

Split families present another challenge for which family therapy is sometimes appropriate. Some families are so split that the parents can barely stand to be in the same room with each other. These are perhaps the families most in need of family therapy. Sometimes the split is still incomplete; that is, the parents have ceased to communicate and share responsibilities with each other but have not yet made a physical separation or divorce. Such families have the most difficulty with learning to manage the behavior of an ADHD child. Family therapy can help such parents see how their conflicts are undermining their parental authority. Individual therapy for each parent and/or marital therapy is often required in addition to family therapy. If a family therapist tries to take on all the issues in a severely split family, the goals of family therapy may be lost in the mess. In divorced or divorcing families, parents frequently have a clearer understanding of the need to find some way to put aside the divorce issues in order to come together on behalf of their child.

In many single-parent families, the control, anger, and acceptance issues are similar in nature but more intense. The single parent's need for support and guidance may be much greater. Children of single-parent families run a higher-than-average risk of developing a conduct disorder, particularly if they are anxious or aggressive and the parent shies from taking control out of fear.

Keith

Keith's mother came to The Children's Hospital of Philadelphia because she was feeling desperate and out of control. Keith had been diagnosed as ADHD years earlier and had received medication and psychotherapy. But the medication was discontinued because Keith had exhibited increasing aggressiveness, anxiety, and sadness when the Ritalin wore off. Since the drug was stopped, Keith's school performance had gotten worse, although he had superior intelligence. Now Keith was eleven years old, and his mother was feeling overwhelmed by his multiple needs and afraid of his aggressiveness. The treatment team decided that Keith needed school evaluations to determine his educational needs and perhaps a medication trial with a different drug. But most important, he needed a therapy program that included his mother so that she could learn to manage his behavior effectively and confidently.

Family conflicts and unresolved anger and hurt can drain energy from parents and children alike, allowing them to lose their sense of power over the situation. The successful management of ADHD requires families to gain a sense of hope that their lives will be better and that answers are within their grasp. Both parents and children need to feel that they have the power to change the ways they are dealing with each other and the ways that other people are dealing with them. Such empowerment comes partly through information, partly through forming helpful relationships, and partly through learning to change behavior. It means choosing battles carefully and not fighting those that cannot be won. It means making wise choices regarding treatment alternatives. And it means learning to protect yourself.

You may want to consult with a family therapist about steps you can take to restore your family's strength. A counselor may be able to help you see things more clearly so that you can get back on course. Your sense of power over the situation is likely to wax and wane over time as your child grows and faces new challenges and as you face new challenges of your own. Thus, you may want to go back to the therapist from time to time for intermittent tune-ups.

ADHD affects so many aspects of family life that it is not unusual for families to need assistance. Family therapy offers many advantages. In addition to giving all family members support and encouragement, it helps the child with ADHD understand that he is not being singled out as abnormal or deviant, and that the whole family is working together to create a better-functioning family unit.

CHAPTER 10

Nontraditional Therapies

Despite the proven effectiveness of many of the medical, behavioral, and educational strategies outlined in the previous chapters, parents of children with ADHD continue to hold out hope for a better and simpler treatment. Some hope for a specific medication that will treat the core symptoms without affecting other aspects of the child's physical or mental health. Others hope for clear-cut behavioral strategies that will "fix" the behavioral deficits without medication. Still others retain the belief that the problems arise from environmental factors such as food-based toxins or inadequate schools, and that if these were fixed, the troublesome behaviors would disappear.

The desire to find a better form of treatment makes perfect sense. In part, it arises from parents' hopes that someone will find a simpler explanation for their children's troubles; that a quick fix will make it all better. In part, it arises from the real inadequacies of current therapeutic approaches. No one really knows the true basis of ADHD children's difficulties. No one knows for sure which forms of therapy will be most effective for any given child.

The search for better treatment alternatives also arises from real parental worries about the safety of medical treatment. In occasional cases, increased anxiety, depression, and

—rarely—psychosis-like illnesses have occurred in individuals taking stimulants. Despite the numerous studies that have shown stimulant medication to be safe and effective for the majority of children, more information is needed about the long-term safety of high doses of stimulants. Alternative therapies appeal to some parents because the standard approaches to therapy don't work for their children or are too time intensive and require the involvement of everyone who comes in contact with the child.

The lack of clarity about the diagnosis and treatment of ADHD not only makes the search for alternatives understandable; it also makes parents susceptible to claims by proponents of numerous unproven therapies. Despite the lack of proof that certain approaches work, stories that report successes with those approaches appear regularly in books, magazines, newspapers, and on television. Parents may tell each other stories of children who experienced dramatic improvements with unproven methods. Parents understandably hope that their child, too, can realize such a benefit. You may be tempted to try a less traditional approach to treatment, either because the standard approaches have not worked or because you object to them for other reasons.

In this chapter we discuss some of the nontraditional therapies that are frequently cited as appropriate for ADHD. Many different nontraditional therapies have been tried, but none has proven to be consistently effective for the majority of children with ADHD. Nevertheless, these methods continue to be studied, and many parents and professionals continue to tout their effectiveness. Here we discuss some factors you may want to think about if you are considering an alternative approach.

In evaluating any form of therapy (including traditional forms of therapy), several factors should be considered. First is the therapy's potential for doing harm. Of course, when a parent is considering a treatment for his child, the most important aspect is its effect on the child's physical health. But harm may come in a variety of forms, and other harmful aspects of a particular treatment should be considered as well. A treatment may be "harmful" in terms of its cost in dollars, time, and/or energy, and this may add strain to a family already stretched to its limits. A treatment method may also be harmful if it falsely raises the family's hopes or frustrates the parents and/or the child. Try to maintain realistic expectations when you are trying an alternative form of therapy.

If a particular form of therapy is associated with a low risk of harm, the next factor to consider is its potential benefits. This is often more difficult to assess. Though some of these strategies have been extensively studied, proof of their effectiveness or lack of effectiveness may be hard to find. An advocate of a certain form of therapy may cite numerous cases in which the therapy proved effective, yet other scientists may refute those claims. Most parents are not in a position to evaluate the design or execution of scientific studies. If one study comes to one conclusion and another study comes to the opposite conclusion, how is a parent to know which to believe? Scientists themselves often disagree about the validity of various studies (although over time a consensus often develops in the scientific community regarding the effectiveness of a particular form of therapy). In the following discussions of various nontraditional therapy alternatives, we will point out what is and is not known about the effectiveness of each approach and some of the experimental problems scientists encounter when they try to gather conclusive evidence. With this information, you should be in a better position to determine whether to pursue a nontraditional therapeutic strategy.

To understand why scientific studies of therapies produce conflicting results, consider the placebo effect. A placebo is a dummy or inactive form of a drug (or other treatment) given to make people think they are receiving treatment when in fact they are not. Scientists often use placebos as controls in experiments. By comparing the results in people who were given the real drug with the results in those given a placebo, scientists can determine whether the drug had a true effect or whether the effect came about for reasons unrelated to the drug's activity, such as a doctor's confidence that it will work or a patient's expectation that he will receive a benefit.

In scientific studies, a significant number of patients show improvement whether or not they have received the treatment. This is called the placebo effect. In other words, some people will improve regardless of the treatment they receive, even though their improvement may *appear* to be related to the treatment. This is why scientists demand controlled studies and why, in the absence of controlled studies, a particular type of treatment may be labeled unproven or ineffective.

DIETARY APPROACHES

The existence of links between diet and behavior has been suggested for decades. Moreover, the existence of links seems so obvious. Certain foods are widely believed to make people feel either more energetic or more sluggish, so it seems reasonable to believe that some foods cause hyperactivity and other behavioral difficulties. In 1974, when Benjamin Feingold published his book *Why Your Child Is Hyperactive,* the positive reaction was swift and widespread. Feingold associations, where parents could learn more about the Feingold diet and share recipes and information, sprang up all around the country. At the same time, other physicians were suggesting other dietary approaches to managing behavior. Scientists tried to study these diets under controlled circumstances, hoping to find an easy explanation for the widespread problem of hyperactivity. But despite all these years of study, most medical professionals do not accept as valid the idea that diet plays a significant role in causing hyperactivity. Nevertheless, some parents still claim that they have successfully controlled their children's hyperactivity through dietary manipulation. Two different approaches are widely advocated.

THE FEINGOLD DIET　The Feingold Diet (also called the Kaiser-Permanente or K-P diet) is based on Feingold's hypothesis that food additives are the cause of hyperactivity in 40 to 50 percent of cases. The Feingold diet eliminates artificial colors and flavors as well as a variety of preservatives, such as BHA and BHT. Feingold also proposed that naturally occurring chemicals called salicylates can produce the symptoms of ADHD. Thus, the diet eliminates all foods that contain natural salicylates, which includes a wide variety of fruits and vegetables.

Eliminating food additives from one's diet is no easy task. Nearly all packaged and processed foods contain chemicals added to increase shelf life or to make the product appear more appetizing. Even some foods that are advertised as "natural" contain chemical additives, which may be "added to the packaging to preserve freshness." Thus, maintaining the Feingold diet means carefully preparing almost all the foods a child eats at home, using fresh, nonprocessed ingredients.

Although many parents report dramatic results from the diet, scientific studies of its effects have been difficult to carry out. Many scientists believe that the diet improves children's behavior primarily because the children are receiving increased attention and because the families adopt a hopeful, optimistic attitude. In laboratory studies, scientists have tried to eliminate the effects of parental and child expectations by "blinding" the subjects as to the presence or absence of additives in the diet. This requires total control of the diet by the scientists; they must provide *all* the food the children eat and be sure that neither the children nor their parents know whether the food contains additives or not. This type of study has been carried out only in a few instances, with inconclusive and discrepant results. One possible explanation for the discrepant results is that there are indeed some children who are sensitive to food additives, but that this is not typical of most hyperactive children, who do not reap significant ongoing benefits from the diet. Further, these studies have been criticized for methodological weaknesses.

So at this time there is little scientific evidence to support the claims of the Feingold diet. For parents who wish to try it, it appears to have a low potential for harm, as long as care is taken to ensure adequate amounts of vitamin C and other nutrients normally obtained from salicylate-containing fruits and vegetables. But parents may want to consider the inconvenience of the diet and weigh its possible benefits against the added stress that may develop. Imposing the diet on children who tend to be oppositional may breed further parent-child conflicts, as the children fight to keep their potato chips and candy bars.

FOOD ALLERGIES AND ELIMINATION DIETS While the Feingold diet focuses on food additives and natural salicylates, other people have proposed that a wide number of foods might produce the symptoms of ADHD in certain susceptible children. Sensitive children are often said to be allergic to certain foods, although the word *allergy* may be a misnomer in this case. *Allergy* refers to a certain type of immunological reaction mediated by specific types of cells and proteins in the body. When an allergic person is exposed to the specific substance (called an allergen) to which he is allergic, a number of characteristic symptoms can occur. If the allergen is a type of pollen, these symptoms may include itchy, watery eyes, a runny nose, and sneezing. If the allergen is a food, the whole body may react, with symptoms ranging from a rash, swelling, and stomach discomfort to increased heart rate and serious difficulty breathing. Food allergies can be definitively diagnosed by an allergist through a variety of laboratory tests. Fish, chocolate, peanuts, strawberries, and milk are some foods that frequently elicit allergies. Many children who have allergies when they are young outgrow them by their teens.

The kind of food sensitivity that some people link to hyperactivity and attention deficit disorders does not work by this allergy mechanism. Nevertheless, these reactions are frequently described as "hidden" or "unsuspected" food allergies. This type of food sensitivity or intolerance is thought to cause tension, fatigue, and a variety of nervous or mental difficulties through some as-yet-unknown mechanism.

Some physicians who call themselves otolaryngic allergists or clinical ecologists claim that they can detect food intolerances by injecting food extracts into a person's arm, then watching for symptoms such as drowsiness or fatigue. Once "allergies" are thus identified, these doctors use weaker injections of the extract, given intravenously or under the tongue, to neutralize the reactions when the foods cannot be avoided. The American Academy of Allergy and Immunology and other medical groups have investigated these claims and concluded that such techniques are ineffective and lack scientific plausibility.

Despite the widespread skepticism about the role of food intolerances in causing the symptoms of ADHD, the explanation still retains many supporters. Since there is no good laboratory test that indicates to which foods a person is sensitive, they advocate the use of dietary manipulation for assessing food sensitivities, or elimination diets. In an elimination diet, all suspected foods are eliminated from a person's diet, then added back individually and gradually so that the reactions to specific foods can be assessed.

Elimination diets take time and a great deal of energy. Usually they begin by eliminating all dairy products; sugar and sugar-containing foods; all products that contain wheat or eggs; all products that contain corn or corn syrup; all products that contain food colors and artificial flavors; chocolate, cola, citrus fruits, fruit juices, peanuts (and peanut oil), beans (including soybean oil and other soy products), honey, maple syrup, and mushrooms. According to the diet plan, the child's symptoms disappear within five to ten days. Then individual items are added back, one per day. If the symptoms return, the food added that day is eliminated from the child's diet.

The most obvious problem with elimination diets is that they are difficult to carry out. Beyond this, there is little scientific evidence to support their use. Nevertheless, some parents report dramatic behavioral improvements when their children strictly follow the diet. It may be that the increased attention given to the children and the strong desire to see some benefit influences either the children's behavior or the parents' perception of improvement.

The lack of scientific support for elimination diets may be a result of the difficulty of carrying out well-controlled dietary studies. Despite this difficulty, in one recent study, a diet that eliminated food additives and several other foodstuffs was shown to improve the behavior of nearly half the children studied, a group of "overactive, inattentive" preschool boys.[11] These boys were selected because they also exhibited allergic symptoms or sleep difficulties, so the results may not apply to nonallergic overactive and inattentive children. But even those children who appeared to benefit from the diet did not become easy to manage. Nevertheless, the study does indicate a clear link between food and behavior and suggested further avenues to explore.

For parents who wish to explore dietary means of improving their child's behavior, the risk appears to be low as long as normal nutritional guidelines are followed.

Megavitamin Therapy

Another nontraditional approach to treating ADHD involves the use of large doses of vitamins. This form of therapy, called orthomolecular psychiatry, presumes that hyperactivity and attention problems are caused by a deficiency of certain chemical substances in the brain, and that these deficiencies can be remedied by oral intake of large quantities of vitamins, usually vitamins C, B_3, and B_6. But again, there is little scientific evidence to support these claims. Some studies have suggested that food additives such as artificial colors and preservatives may cause hyperactivity by blocking the action of pyridoxine (vitamin B_6), and that supplementation with B_6 may counteract the negative effects of these additives. But this theory has yet to be widely tested to prove either the effectiveness or safety of treatment based on it. Some vitamins, notably vitamins A, B_6, and D, can be toxic when taken in high doses, and the safety of large doses of other vitamins also remains in question. Therefore, most medical professionals oppose the use of megavitamin therapy until effectiveness and safety can be firmly established.

SENSORY INTEGRATION THERAPY

Another nontraditional approach that is popular among some health professionals—primarily occupational therapists—is sensory integration (SI) therapy. The idea behind SI therapy is that some children have neurological difficulties that affect their ability to organize and interpret incoming sensory input. Such children may exhibit a variety of learning and behavioral problems, including overactivity, disorganization, learning difficulties, and oversensitivity to touch. Though SI therapy has had success in improving the behavior and learning ability of some children with certain types of developmental disabilities such as autism and mental retardation, its use among children with ADHD remains controversial.

SI therapy first defines the nature of a child's SI dysfunction, then designs a series of individualized sensory-oriented activities aimed at correcting the problem. For example, some children who exhibit increased motor activity have difficulty processing tactile information because they are oversensitive to light touch. Consequently they frequently feel physically uncomfortable and as a result appear fidgety and restless. SI therapy defines this problem, then designs activities in which carefully selected and controlled tactile stimulation is necessary to successfully complete some task. The SI therapist adjusts the amount of tactile stimulation over time as a way of conditioning the person to tolerate such stimulation more easily. SI therapy usually involves hour-long sessions for several weeks or months.

The few treatment trials in which SI therapy has been used for specific learning disabilities and learning difficulties have not had promising results. Although some studies have suggested that SI produced a benefit, they have been criticized for methodological problems. As you might expect, it is difficult to establish an effective placebo control for this type of therapy. In an uncontrolled trial that favorably compared the effects of SI therapy to the effects of no therapy at all, the child might benefit simply from the one-on-one therapy session rather than from the SI exercises themselves. In some studies that have attempted to use controls, such as one-on-one sessions without SI exercises, SI therapy has not been shown to be beneficial. So at this time, SI therapy is not thought to be effective for children with ADHD. Still, further evaluation of SI therapy is needed to determine whether a certain subgroup of children who have both ADHD and SI dysfunction might benefit from it.

RELAXATION AND BIOFEEDBACK

Biofeedback trains people to control their bodily processes that are not normally under voluntary control. The person is hooked up to an electronic device that measures a physiological function such as muscle tension or blood pressure. When the person successfully lowers his blood pressure or reduces his muscle tension, the machine sounds a tone that tells him of his success. This feedback presumably acts as a positive reinforcer that helps the person learn to consciously control that bodily function.

Biofeedback training has been promoted by some therapists as a method for teaching children with ADHD to relax. Presumably, relaxation would allow the children to function better in the classroom, both behaviorally and academically. Studies of the effects of biofeedback training on children with ADHD have suggested that many of these children can learn to relax better. But whether they can apply that skill outside of the laboratory environment remains in question. Some studies have indicated that children's academic performance and classroom behavior can be substantially improved and that they may even be able to discontinue medication after a period of biofeedback training. But other studies have failed to substantiate that biofeedback's benefits continue outside of the laboratory. Thus, at this time, there is little evidence to support the contention that biofeedback training is a realistic alternative for the treatment of ADHD. At the same time, however, it presents very little risk and may offer some benefits in terms of stress reduction, even if its effects on ADHD are not significant.

CHIROPRACTIC MANIPULATION

Chiropractors believe that many diseases—including mental illnesses and some behavioral and learning disorders—are caused by misaligned vertebrae that interfere with proper nerve function. Therefore, they attempt to treat disease through spinal manipulation. Chiropractic is widely accepted as a useful therapy for the treatment of pain and disorders of the joints and muscles. But its usefulness in treating mental and behavioral disorders remains controversial. Like some of the therapy methods already discussed, controlled trials are difficult to accomplish with chiropractic. Chiropractic has been promoted as a possible nondrug intervention for ADHD, but its effectiveness has not been clearly established at this time.

An offshoot of chiropractic called neural organization technique (NOT) has also been promoted as a cure for dyslexia and learning disabilities. Chiropractors who practice NOT manipulate the skull as well as the spine, claiming that misaligned skull bones adversely affect brain function. In addition, they claim that they can diagnose a child's problems in a few minutes simply by assessing the strength of various muscles. NOT has become very controversial in some areas. Though some parents claim that it has worked wonders for their children, many children and parents report that it involves extreme levels of pain. Some parents feel that NOT produced other negative side effects as well, causing their children to become moody, aggressive, and anxious. No good scientific studies have attested to the effectiveness of NOT. This lack of proof, combined with NOT's potential to cause pain and possibly injury, strongly suggests that it is a therapy to be avoided.

OTHER NONTRADITIONAL THERAPIES

This chapter has not presented all the nontraditional forms of therapy that may be suggested as potentially beneficial for your child. New ideas and new treatments continue to be offered in the search for better alternatives. When they are new, most treatments are viewed as controversial. Some remain controversial even after many years of study. In general, we feel that your child has the best chance for success if you pursue traditional methods under the guidance of a caring, knowledgeable professional. But if you have tried the traditional approaches and your child does not seem to be making sufficient progress, you may wish to try one of these other methods, preferably in consultation with a respected professional. If a nontraditional approach works for your child and does not have the potential to harm him, it would appear sensible to continue with it. If you are considering a nontraditional approach, find out as much as you can about it before you start. Talk to other people who have tried it, consider both the pluses and minuses, and try to set realistic expectations.

PART III
Living with ADHD

CHAPTER 11

Taking Care of Your Child's Social and Emotional Needs

Although the management of ADHD focuses primarily on alleviating children's problems in the classroom and at home, their difficulties may range far beyond those situations. In fact, possibly the greatest problems that ADHD children face are in the areas of their own self-esteem and their peer relationships. The core symptoms of ADHD set children up to experience failure and to face criticism and rejection. And while medication, behavior therapy, and educational intervention are designed to address the core symptoms, they may not be adequate to fix the damage done to the child's internal sense of mastery and competence. As ADHD children grow and face new challenges, their social and emotional difficulties often mount.

In this chapter, we discuss some of the social and emotional issues that trouble children with ADHD. There are no easy prescriptions for guarding against these problems, just as there are no easy explanations for why one child is more troubled than another. All the efforts you make toward improving your child's success in school and his ability to get along better with his family members, teachers, and friends will have multiple benefits as he begins to internalize a sense of self-confidence and success. Some of the steps you take will be small; others will require you to make more significant changes in the way your family operates.

SELF-ESTEEM

Everyone seems to be talking about self-esteem these days: how to get it, how to keep it, and what damages it. It is easy to figure out how self-esteem is damaged in ADHD children. These are children who experience failure at an early age, who rarely feel that they fit in or are accepted by those around them, and who find themselves entangled in so many bouts of hostility with their parents that they miss out on hugs and other signs of affection that would reassure them of their parents' love. But these are not the only sources of damage to self-esteem that ADHD children face. Even when they are quite young, before they have been beaten down by a sense of failure, many ADHD children recognize that they are "different." They are often heard to say "No one likes me." When they are old enough to reflect on their childhood, many people with ADHD report that they always felt disconnected, as if they were missing out on much of what was going on around them. They describe constant feelings of restlessness, insecurity, and irritability. Many felt ashamed at being so impulsive, so quick to fly off the handle.

The term *self-esteem* refers to a number of hard-to-define qualities, such as a person's sense of mastery and competence, self-confidence, and an appreciation and acceptance of himself. In other words, it refers to how well a person likes himself. Most people like some things about themselves and don't like others, and these feelings may change over time.

Self-esteem arises from any number of sources. In the early years, family love and acceptance and success at mastering skills are the most important sources of children's self-esteem. As they get older, peer acceptance and school performance play important roles as well. When children do poorly in school, they sometimes can compensate and retain a good

Eddie

Eight-year-old Eddie told his parents that no one at school liked him. Before he started taking Ritalin, he had a lot of behavior problems both at home and at school, some aggressiveness, and impulsivity. The drug seemed to help a great deal, but his difficult behaviors resurfaced when it wore off. His teacher told his parents that Eddie interacted well with the other children on a one-to-one basis, but that he liked to clown around in a group and did not know when to stop. The other children found his behavior annoying, got mad at him, and left him out of their games. In addition, Eddie had some motor difficulties and lacked confidence on the playground. He said he was always the last person chosen when the class picked teams. Eddie's ADHD symptoms clearly affected his self-esteem.

sense of self-esteem if they are good at sports, physically attractive, or socially skilled.

Many of the management strategies you may already be using are geared to improving your child's success in school and his ability to get along well with his peers. These measures will also help nourish his self-esteem. In addition, through family therapy, you may be working on resolving conflicts that contribute to your child's low self-esteem. Even if you are not in therapy, there are a number of steps you can take to strengthen your family's functioning as well as your child's inner strength. First, you and your child must learn and accept that having ADHD does not mean that he is "defective." His specific difficulties must be dealt with directly, without worry about their deeper significance. If your child throws tantrums or is destructive, that behavior must be controlled before the reasons for it can be explored.

IMPROVING YOUR CHILD'S SELF-CONFIDENCE AND MASTERY Families should also try to instill in the child a sense that he has the ability to overcome his problems. This can be problematic if the child is taking medication. He may attribute his success to the drugs rather than to his own accomplishments. As parents, you must reinforce to your child that the drugs help him focus better and maintain control so that *he* can use his natural abilities more successfully. Further, you should reward your child's efforts and use language that shows him that you attribute his success to his efforts.

Nurture your child's strengths; this will help diminish the importance of his weaknesses. Acknowledge his accomplishments, and try to make little fuss over his failures. You may even find that strengths lie behind his troublesome behavior. For instance, if your child continually tests the limits with you or his teachers, appreciate the fact that this ability will help him find his way through any system of obstacles he may encounter. This doesn't mean that you should encourage him to test or defy you, but you may want to acknowledge to him that this characteristic, which presents much difficulty for him in some situations, can become a strength in other situations if he can learn to channel his assertiveness at the right times.

Part of nurturing self-esteem involves altering your and your child's expectations and setting realistic, attainable goals. This doesn't necessarily mean you lower your overall expectations. If your child is of high intelligence, you need not assume that he will never achieve at his intellectual level, but you may need to adjust your expectations for certain aspects of his achievement. Perhaps he will not do well in subjects that require sustained attention to detail, such as advanced mathematics. But he may excel in areas that require more creative and flexible thinking. Of course, you will want to work on building his abilities in his weaker areas, but do so without losing sight of his strengths. If he has difficulty in staying organized and planning strategy, for instance, help him learn skills that will make up for this weakness even as you help him institute structures that will make his lack of organization less troublesome. One ADHD child, Joe, continually forgot to bring his homework assignments home after school. His mother tried to revoke his privileges as a way of modifying his behavior, but he continued to forget. When she realized that he was not forgetting maliciously, she tried a different strategy: she made up a checklist of supplies he needed to remember each day and asked his teacher to help him go over it before he left school. By doing this, she lowered her expectations, in that she no longer expected him to be able to remember his schoolwork. But she also helped him compensate for his weakness by teaching him an alternative strategy, and she alleviated some of the negative consequences that would have ensued (such as not having the work done the next day).

Setting realistic expectations helps your child achieve feelings of competency and mastery. In addition, it can help relieve some of your worries, anxieties, and disappointments. You will be able to take pride in your child's small accomplishments rather than focusing on what he has not done. That, in turn, bolsters your child's self-confidence, which helps him function more effectively, and so on.

HELPING YOUR CHILD FEEL LOVED AND ACCEPTED The other major part of self-esteem is one's sense of being loved and accepted. You no doubt love your child; otherwise you would not be reading this book. But the conflicts between you may make your expressions of that love infrequent in comparison with your expressions of exasperation, frustration, and hostility. If you have other children, you may feel guilty about the amount of attention you give to your ADHD child, and therefore you may spend more of your leisure time and "fun" energy with his brothers and sisters. Consequently, your children may be getting equivalent amounts of attention, but the child with ADHD is getting it primarily through negative and angry interactions. This can reinforce to him that he is "bad" or unloved and can make him feel like a scapegoat for all the negative interactions in the family. Try to prevent this from happening by concentrating on doing fun things with your ADHD child. Make a special effort to cultivate positive interactions with him, and be alert for times when you can give him positive attention. Try to get him out of the scapegoat role.

Early intervention can help prevent low self-esteem from developing in very young children, who have not been beaten down by many years of failure and criticism. With older children, however, low self-esteem is not easily reversed. Older children's sense of failure and disappointment often becomes so deeply entrenched in their self-image that change is slow. Accepting this may help you to avoid giving up too quickly on your older child, his teacher, or yourself.

PEER RELATIONSHIPS

Many children with ADHD have difficulty getting along with other children at school, on the playground, and elsewhere. Some peer problems take the form of bullying: either the child himself is aggressive and bullying, or he is the object of a bully's attentions, a "whipping boy." Other ADHD children simply have difficulty making and keeping friends. Either way, ADHD children's problems with peer relationships may be among the most significant aspects of their disorder. Many studies have shown that children with poor social skills are much more likely to experience continuing problems as they move into adolescence and adulthood. Many aggressive, bullying children do not outgrow their antisocial behaviors; they have a much higher incidence of juvenile delinquency, criminality, and substance abuse. Likewise, rejected or disliked children are at an increased risk of engaging in antisocial behavior and having social and psychological problems that arise from their low self-esteem.

The core symptoms of ADHD—impulsivity, overactivity, and inattention—give rise to many of the peer problems that children with ADHD have. Their impulsivity may lead them to lash out in an aggressive way when they are challenged or when they become angry. Their overactivity may put them at odds with children who prefer a slower pace. Their inattention may create difficulties when they are playing games that involve following rules or keeping track of what is happening.

In addition to the problems that arise from the core symptoms, children with ADHD frequently display other behaviors that create roadblocks when they try to make friends. Some are overly demanding of attention and, as a result, act out in obnoxious, unpleasant ways. Others have a low frustration tolerance and have difficulty making transitions from one activity to another; both these characteristics may make other children reluctant to establish friendships with them. Some have learning disabilities or motor coordination problems that set them up to be teased or that interfere with their ability to interact normally with other children. And many have poor social perception skills, which means that they misread subtle social cues, and poor social judgment, which leads them to act inappropriately at times.

Treatment of the core symptoms may relieve the difficulties some children experience in their peer relationships. But other ADHD children need social guidance, either social-skills training or help in finding social situations that will encourage rather than discourage appropriate peer interactions. If your child is having difficulty making friends or getting along with other children at school, do not ignore the problems; they generally will not go away on their own. How you should intervene is less than clear. Researchers have not clearly identified a path that leads to better social skills. But experience with hundreds of children with ADHD has suggested some avenues that may be useful.

Social-skills training sometimes takes place in organized groups or classes, as discussed in chapter 7. Unfortunately, such classes have not proved useful for many children with ADHD. Even when they learn to behave appropriately in the artificial environment of the class, they often cannot apply those skills in natural settings, such as on the playground.

Much of what children learn about appropriate social interactions comes from their parents at home, from teachers at school, from other adults in various environments, and from other children in the play yard. As a parent, you may be able to structure your child's environment to maximize his likelihood of developing good social skills. For a young child, for example, you might organize a small play group at home. For an older child, you might allow your child to invite over one friend at a time. Think carefully about who you allow to come over; children with good social skills may be able to model for your child how to act appropriately. In addition, plan play activities that offer structure to the children's interactions. Children with ADHD often have great difficulty controlling their impulsiveness and overactivity when there is no structure for them to follow. You may want to remain present during structured playtime to supervise the activities. Talk with your child ahead of time about exactly what you expect of him. If he is bossy, explain to him that you would like him to let his friend go *first* in a game. Keep the playtime short at first, monitor the children as they play, and reward your child's appropriate behavior, either unobtrusively during play or sometime shortly afterward. If hostilities begin to arise, intervene early: stop the aggression before it has a chance to develop. You may want to limit the time when your child is "on his own" in the neighborhood without guidance or supervision.

For children who have few or no friends, parents may be able to identify one or two children with whom they could develop friendships. Research has shown that children's abilities to function socially are greatly enhanced if they have only one reciprocal friend, compared with children who have no reciprocal friends. Reciprocal friends are those who like each other. Even just one reciprocal friend can help a child develop better social skills, which in turn can affect his self-esteem and happiness.

You can help your child nurture friendships in a variety of ways. For instance, you can serve as a model from which your child can learn how to develop a friendship. Be nice to your child's friends, and go out of your way to make the friends feel welcome in your home. Try to make your home a fun place to come to so that other children want to come over. These steps not only demonstrate to your child appropriate ways of interacting, they can help compensate for his social weaknesses. You cannot make friends for your child, but you may be able to encourage the kinds of interactions that will help your child establish friendships.

When children's peer problems occur primarily at school—teasing, fighting, or rejection on the playground—parents need to enlist the help of school personnel. Bring your concerns to the attention of your child's teacher, guidance counselor, or principal, or bring in a professional who can work with the school to set up appropriate interventions. For example, a guidance counselor may be able to set up a social-skills training group in the school or some social problem-solving sessions. Ideally, these groups include both ADHD children and children who either purposely or inadvertently are antagonizing the impulsive child. You should also plan for generalization. Have the counselor consult with your child's teachers on how to cue and reinforce appropriate social skills.

Outside-the-classroom activities—such as recess, lunch, or assemblies—may be particularly problematic for children with ADHD, but little attention is usually given to relieving difficulties there. Nonetheless, these areas are receiving increased scrutiny from behavioral scientists. They have shown that aggression on the playground can be significantly reduced merely by organizing playground activities rather than leaving the children to their own unorganized, unstructured play. Instituting clear and consistent consequences for misbehavior on the bus or in the cafeteria can reduce disruptions there. This line of research suggests that intervention for ADHD may involve training teachers, playground and cafeteria aides, and bus drivers in appropriate behavior-management strategies. Unfortunately, few schools are taking this approach at the present time.

EXTRACURRICULAR ACTIVITIES

As children get older, their social life increasingly extends beyond the home and the classroom. Children with ADHD, like other children, gain multiple benefits from these extracurricular activities, which offer them a chance to develop their social, physical, and intellectual skills and build friendships. These benefits can dramatically enhance children's self-esteem and overall sense of happiness. But as in other aspects of ADHD children's lives, care must be taken to ensure that the challenges are not insurmountable and that they will not come away feeling defeated. All parents hope their children will be successful in whatever activities they pursue, and all parents worry that failure will damage their children's sense of self. Parents of children with ADHD have an increased set of worries since their children come to extracurricular activities with several strikes against them. While most children with ADHD can participate in most of the activities they choose, in some cases taking special steps can maximize their chances for success.

The most important factor to consider when helping children choose extracurricular activities is to fit the activities to their interests and talents. Generally, organized group activities supervised by an adult are better for children with ADHD than are peer-mediated activities. Children with ADHD often have trouble taking turns and following rules, and they tend to respond better to adult direction than to criticism from their peers. When children are in charge, some ADHD children become bossy and aggressive, while others withdraw completely. Adults can often intervene before the situation becomes problematic. Examples of adult-organized activities include scouts, youth groups sponsored by churches, synagogues, or community centers, and sports.

When it comes to sports, several factors must be kept in mind. First, some children with ADHD are clumsy and uncoordinated. But they should still be encouraged to participate in physical activity. Physical well-being can have a dramatic impact on their self-esteem. Sports also offer excellent opportunities to hone social skills, learn to take turns, and have fun. Generally, less competitive sports such as T-ball and swimming are best unless a child is very athletic. Coach selection can play an important role in your child's success. If you can find a coach who is willing to work with an inattentive child and who is patient, quick to reward effort, and more interested in teaching children to play and have fun than in winning, the likelihood of your child's success rises greatly.

Athletic and coordinated children with ADHD are another story altogether. For such children, sports can be their saving grace, the aspect of their lives that enhances their self-esteem even when they are unsuccessful in other areas such as school. This was the case with ten-year-old Scott, who was an especially accomplished swimmer. Generally, children with ADHD do better in individual-performance sports such as tennis, swimming, and track than in team sports. Soccer, basketball, hockey, and football are difficult for several reasons. First, they require a high degree of concentration on the game even when the individual is not directly involved. Children with ADHD often have trouble staying focused. Second, many ADHD children have trouble following rules and taking turns—two important aspects of team sports. Third, these sports require team members to work together, so a lapse of attentiveness on the part of one child may make his whole team suffer and criticize him as a result. Fourth, these sports tend to be highly competitive, which can be problematic for some ADHD children, especially younger children. This is not to say that children should be discouraged from playing team sports if they choose them. A particular child's success depends to a great extent on how motivated he is. But he may need extra help in staying focused and attentive during games.

Baseball is of intermediate difficulty for ADHD children. Although it is technically a team sport, most of the game really centers on the individual battle between the batter and the pitcher. Thus, when a child with ADHD is at bat, he may have little difficulty staying focused and alert, but out in left field, far from the center of attention, the same child may have great difficulty concentrating on the game.

For ADHD children who are athletic and highly motivated to play competitive sports but who have difficulty staying focused, the solution may be to use stimulant medication during the sports activity. In one recent study, the effects of Ritalin on eight-to-ten-year-old children playing baseball were assessed.[12] The drug did not affect the children's skills —that is, they were able to hit and throw as well (or as poorly) as they did without the medication. But it did enhance their ability to pay attention to the game. The authors surmised that increased attentiveness could pay off for ADHD children in terms of their peer relations because other team members are more accepting of their mistakes if they appear to be trying, rather than staring off into space. Thus, if your child chooses to participate in competitive sports, consider giving him an afternoon or weekend dose of medication on those days.

In conclusion, having ADHD should not limit the activities in which your child can participate. But your child is more likely to be successful in some types of activities than in others. If his ADHD-related difficulties are causing problems in his social activities, there are steps you can take to relieve those difficulties, including using stimulant medication at times when your child would normally be drug-free. As your child gets older, he may be able to judge for himself whether he functions better with or without medication.

CHAPTER 12

Growing Up with ADHD

Although ADHD is still thought of primarily as a children's disorder, it appears that for nearly half of ADHD children, symptoms persist through adolescence and into adulthood. The problems may change over time: hyperactivity may decline, while impulsivity and inattention take on new significance. As new pressures arise, the focus of attention may shift from academics to social situations. Expectations may change as parents and teachers—and later, co-workers and spouses—become less tolerant of impulsive and inattentive behaviors. Compensatory strategies that work well for elementary-age children may be inadequate when those children reach high school, and they may be completely useless in the adult years. In this chapter we discuss the changing problems of the adolescent and adult with ADHD. Parents of ADHD children often remember the old adage "Little kids, little problems; big kids, big problems." They approach their children's teenage years with trepidation. While this chapter is not meant to allay all those fears, its message is that you can help your child negotiate adolescence and prepare him for a bright future.

PROGNOSIS

No one can accurately predict the outcome for an individual child with ADHD. But researchers have studied outcome in large numbers of ADHD children. In 1986, Gabrielle Weiss and Lily Trokenberg Hechtman reported on their own long-term studies of hyperactive children as well as on the research of others who have studied long-term outcome.[13] They concluded that about half of those studied continued to have problems as adults. These problems included impulsive personality traits, frequent accidents, frequent moves from one place to another, less education, and a lower self-concept. Even those who had fairly good outcomes often complained of restlessness, poor concentration, impulsivity, and explosiveness.

Other studies have supported and extended Weiss and Hechtman's conclusions. Rachel Gittelman Klein and her colleagues found that nearly 70 percent of children diagnosed with hyperactivity or attention deficit disorder retained symptoms into early adolescence; about half of them (35 percent) continued to warrant a diagnosis of ADHD as young adults.[14] More important, of those who continued to be troubled by their symptoms, nearly half displayed antisocial disorders such as truancy, stealing, serious lying, and aggression, and almost a third were drug abusers. It is important to remember that these people were originally diagnosed years ago and probably did not receive the multiple types of treatment interventions that children receive now.

Though these findings seem discouraging, good news was reported as well. Salvatore Mannuzza, working with Klein, studied outcome in adolescents and young adults who had been diagnosed as hyperactive during childhood but who did not continue to have difficulties later in life.[15] Though this group of people reported being more distractible and hyperactive than others and said they had more trouble concentrating, they appeared to function fairly well. In comparison with a group of nonhyperactive people, they had no significantly higher incidence of school failure, dropping out, conduct problems, or drug or alcohol use.

Thus, it appears that many people continue to be troubled by the symptoms of ADHD but that many are also able to leave the disorder behind, either because the symptoms diminish over time or because they learn to compensate for their difficulties. This conclusion poses two important questions: First, is there any way to predict which children will continue to have difficulties beyond childhood? Second, does treatment help prevent these difficulties from continuing?

Some research has suggested that children with clear-cut aggression are more likely than nonaggressive children to retain symptoms of ADHD and antisocial behaviors into adolescence and adulthood. But even nonaggressive children with ADHD develop conduct disorders more often than do normal children. Thus, while aggression increases the likelihood of poor outcome, other factors are also at work, including the social, psychological, emotional, and intellectual aspects of a child's life. For instance, heightened parent-child conflict predisposes children to long-term problems, but above-average intelligence makes a positive outcome more likely, probably because these children are better able to compensate for their academic weaknesses. Likewise, other positive aspects of a child's life may contribute to a good outcome. A child who is good at sports, very popular, or very attractive may have a better-than-average chance of retaining a strong sense of self-esteem, which can result in better overall functioning later in life.

In addition, treatment may help prevent ongoing problems. In chapter 4, we discussed the work of James Satterfield and his colleagues, who have investigated strategies for preventing delinquency in hyperactive boys. Satterfield showed that long-term multimodal treatment, consisting of medication and intensive behavioral-psychological therapy, lowered the incidence of arrests and imprisonments, compared with drug treatment alone.

Parents often worry that giving their child stimulant medication for hyperactivity will set him up to be a drug abuser later in life. But in fact the opposite may be true. Several studies have shown that stimulants do not increase the risk for drug abuse. Furthermore, by controlling some of the troublesome symptoms, stimulants may lower the incidence of secondary problems that commonly occur in children with ADHD, such as anxiety, depression, and low self-esteem. As a consequence, medicated children may be able to avoid some of the social and emotional stressors that can later lead to substance abuse.

In conclusion, it appears that some children are more predisposed to having continued problems in adolescence and adulthood than others, but the outcome is neither predictable nor predetermined. Many children learn to compensate for their difficulties; some even excel as a result of the coping skills they learn. You may remember Joel from this book's introduction, for example, whose compensatory skills helped him through medical school and continued to help him juggle many of his adult responsibilities. His own struggle with learning disabilities and ADD also gave him an appreciation of the difficulties that people face and helped instill in him a strong sense of compassion.

The treatment methods outlined in this book can help you maximize your child's chances of becoming a happy, successful, and well-functioning adult. But you, as well as your child, must work to achieve that goal. When formerly hyperactive children are asked what helped them the most, many say that it was having someone who believed in them: an accepting and supportive parent, teacher, or other adult. In addition, many of those who mastered a certain skill or developed expertise in a specific field grew up with stronger self-concepts and as a result were more successful.

So far in this chapter, we have discussed the prognosis for ADHD children in terms of percentages. But as we saw in chapter 1, ADHD is not an either/or proposition. People do not simply have or not have ADHD. Rather, ADHD-like symptoms that people have may create more or less difficulty for them, depending on many factors. Likewise, for ADHD adolescents and adults, the extent of difficulty that persisting symptoms create varies depending on the severity of the symptoms and other facets of their lives. In the rest of this chapter, we focus on some of the problems that frequently trouble people with ADHD as they move into adolescence and adulthood. In addition, we discuss the impact of these continuing problems on other family members.

The Adolescent with ADHD

Although ADHD may be diagnosed as early as the preschool years, the diagnosis typically comes later, when problems in school become too significant to be ignored. This is particularly true of children for whom overactivity is not a major problem and for those who have neither learning disabilities nor a conduct disorder. Overall, the average age of diagnosis is nine years. Many children who do receive a diagnosis of ADHD in early childhood have problems that are sufficiently mild that they receive little or no treatment aimed at preventing them from getting worse. Thus, children with ADHD often reach adolescence with multiple areas of difficulty that have built up over the years to become major problems. A child who performs at a slightly below average academic level for a number of years may grow up to be a teenager with significant skill deficits. On top of that, he may have suffered years of frustration from being told he should, or could, do better, and he may have developed a deeply felt sense of failure.

This is not to say that early diagnosis and treatment entirely prevent problems from continuing in adolescence. Whether children receive early and appropriate treatment or not, adolescence commonly brings them a new set of difficulties and stressors and thus requires a reevaluation of management strategies. Amy, for example, was diagnosed with ADD in first grade and has taken stimulants since that time. She has maintained average grades in school, but her poor social skills are becoming more and more troublesome as she gets older. This is frequently the case in girls with ADHD, as adolescence brings particularly heavy social pressures. Now age twelve, Amy needs a reevaluation of her medication regimen and possibly more intensive social-skills and behavior therapy.

Many of the problems seen in adolescents with ADHD resemble those seen in "normal" teenagers. Generally, adolescents are trying to put their childhood behind them. They want more independence, freedom, and autonomy. They reject parental authority, and they rebel against expectations. Their way of thinking about the world changes, and their bodies change, too, contributing to dramatic mood swings and emotional outbursts. Unfortunately, for children with ADHD, inattention, impulsivity, and other ADHD-related symptoms combine with the normal adolescent pressures to create a volatile mix. In comparison to other children, they may be less able to handle increased independence. They tend to make impulsive rather than reasoned decisions, which can get them into trouble with drugs, sex, and other temptations of adolescence. Parent-child conflicts may increase to the point of open hostility.

In junior high and high school, increasing demands are placed on these children's academic skills. They need to pay more attention to details, to plan and strategize more effectively, and to complete more work. They are expected to be able to work more independently, with less assistance from teachers and parents. In other words, adolescence hits children with a double dose of difficulty: just at the time when they may be most vulnerable and unsteady, demands and expectations placed on them go up.

TREATING ADHD IN ADOLESCENTS Although adolescence is a time when behavioral problems are often at a peak, it is also a time when many parents and physicians choose to discontinue stimulant medication, even when it was an effective treatment in childhood. They do this even though stimulants have been shown to be as effective for adolescents and adults as they are for children. But other factors often argue against continuing the drugs. First, although the drugs given for ADHD do not predispose children to drug abuse, adolescence is a time when significant numbers of teenagers, with ADHD and without ADHD, experiment with drugs. Since stimulants taken in relatively large quantities or intravenously can produce feelings of euphoria, they are subject to abuse. Therefore, a doctor may choose to try another type of drug, such as an antidepressant or clonidine, which does not produce pleasurable feelings and thus is not likely to be abused.

A second reason for altering the medication regimen of teenagers is their increased academic and social demands. Late nights spent doing homework and more frequent and lengthy social activities may mean that round-the-clock, everyday medication is necessary. The ups and downs associated with Ritalin therapy may add too much stress to adolescents who already feel off balance.

The third reason for altering the medication regimen is that many teenagers see the regimen as something imposed by parents, and thus they reject it simply as a way of rejecting parental authority. If medication is to be used for a teenager, his cooperation must be obtained. He must see it as something that can help him stay in control, rather than as something used to control him. If a teenager is allowed to experience a favorite activity both on and off the medication, the benefits may become more apparent to him. For example, if he participates in a football game on medication, he may appreciate that it helps him stay focused on the game and decreases conflict with his coach or teammates.

But medication is not always the primary treatment approach for adolescents with ADHD. When medication is contraindicated, treatment may involve a combination of counseling and educational intervention, including remedial help for delayed skills. And always, adolescents must actively participate in their own treatment. They are old enough to understand and appreciate their difficulties, and they should be able to verbalize their feelings to a greater extent than they could as children. A child with ADHD may have expressed his anger and frustration by throwing a tantrum, hitting, or destroying something, but as an adolescent he can learn to express those feelings verbally.

While some factors argue against medicating adolescents, some teenagers who managed without medication in childhood find that the increased demands they face in high school and the internal changes in their bodies increase their need for medication. Some who were medicated as children choose to continue it for similar reasons. This was the case for thirteen-year-old Aaron. His decision to continue medication was a difficult one for him and his parents to make, as it brought up feelings that somehow they had failed in not being able to "beat" the disorder. And it dashed their hopes that Aaron would "outgrow" his problems.

Probably the most significant problem area for adolescents with ADHD is self-esteem. Young children gain much of their self-esteem through positive parent-child interactions, but adolescents look to their performance academically, socially, athletically, or in other areas for their sense of self-confidence and self-worth. Thus, adolescents with ADHD who have experienced chronic failure or underachievement may have deeply ingrained low self-esteem. In chapter 11 we discussed ways you can help build your child's self-esteem; for an adolescent whose self-esteem is already badly damaged, family or individual therapy may be needed to educate the person about the nature of his disorder, help him build realistic expectations and goals, and help him deal with bottled-up anger and frustration.

Parents may also need some added support while their child is a teenager. Defiance and disobedience can explode into open hostility at this time. Even parents who have developed good parenting skills over the years may find themselves at a loss to deal with their child. Further, parents often find themselves increasingly depressed when they realize that the problems did not go away when their child reached puberty. This may be a time when expectations need to be reevaluated, possibly through another round of family therapy. Sometimes parents simply feel that they need advice from a professional regarding specific aspects of their children's lives. For instance, parents may wonder whether their impulsive and distractible sixteen-year-old can drive safely. In some cases, the doctor may recommend that the child drive only when medicated. But by and large, doctors have few clear answers for parents of adolescents with ADHD. Little research has been conducted regarding treatment alternatives among these children. Nor is much known about the effects of long-term stimulant treatment.

Adults with ADHD

Only in the past few years has ADHD been recognized as a long-term, chronic condition that may persist throughout a person's life. In addition, it has only been some twenty years since inattention was identified as a problem of equal importance to hyperactivity. Thus, many adults who today have what doctors would describe as residual ADHD may not have been diagnosed as children because they were not hyperactive. Or, for those who were hyperactive as young children, their problems may have been ignored in later years under the presumption that they had disappeared. Those who exhibit coexisting conduct disorders, aggression, or antisocial behaviors may have been tagged as delinquent, deviant, or criminal; but those with milder symptoms may have simply fallen through the cracks. Now in their thirties, forties, and fifties, some of them are being diagnosed and treated.

Not only do adults with ADHD exhibit the core symptoms of the disorder, especially inattention and impulsivity; they frequently display other symptoms commonly seen in children with ADHD. Many have dramatic mood swings, short and hot tempers, a low frustration tolerance, and significant problems with organization and planning. They often have significant secondary problems as well. The problems associated with ADHD dramatically influence adults' sense of themselves and their ability to establish meaningful relationships. Adults with ADHD also tend to have lower on-the-job performance ratings.

In college or at work, inattention and distractibility may cause people with ADHD to have trouble completing projects and activities. They may forget important appointments and commitments. These problems, combined with low frustration tolerance, disorganization, and poor planning skills, may lead adults with ADHD to change jobs frequently. As a result, they may feel constantly discouraged about their inability to achieve the level of success they expect.

In social situations, ADHD symptoms lead adults to problems in establishing and maintaining relationships, especially close ones. Significant others may complain that such a person doesn't listen or pay attention, always seems preoccupied, acts irresponsibly, and cannot be depended on. As a result, the ADHD person often feels either guilty or angry and misunderstood. Significant others sometimes switch to an overfunctioning role, in which they try to take care of all the details that the person with ADHD seems unable to manage. In this case, the person with ADHD may end up even more incapacitated by his weaknesses and with a further diminished sense of self-worth. The overfunctioning helpmate may seethe with anger about her increasing responsibilities. All in all, it makes for a troubled relationship.

Adults diagnosed with ADHD often experience initial feelings of relief at finally having an explanation for their difficulties. This may be followed by tremendous regret, anger, and resentment for the years during which they were labeled bad, irresponsible, unreliable, a failure, and worse. In addition to having these mixed-up feelings of relief and anger, many diagnosed adults are confused about how the diagnosis affects their perception of themselves. On the one hand, a diagnosis may allow a person to let himself off the hook for some of his difficulties. But it may also increase his doubts about his ability to cope with problems.

Some adults are diagnosed with ADHD after learning of their children's diagnosis. This can be especially painful for a parent (usually a father) who must cope not only with the typical unsettling feelings but with the guilt of having passed the disorder on to his child. He may overidentify with the child and thus have difficulty exerting effective parental control. On top of that, he may have to deal with his spouse's chronic anger at both him and the child.

Because of these compounding problems in adults with ADHD, treatment may need to be focused in several directions. Some of the same strategies that are useful with children and adolescents may also be useful with adults. In particular, stimulants appear to have similar effects on adults as they do on children, increasing their ability to focus attention and decreasing fidgetiness.

The major focus of adult treatment, however, should be to rebuild confidence and self-esteem. These adults need to gain a sense of competence, and they can do this by setting realistic goals for themselves and then fulfilling them. Often this involves relearning how to structure their time and organize their lives. Therapy should be directed at helping ADHD adults understand and confront behaviors that have led to difficulties: avoidance of responsibility, avoidance of commitment, and avoidance of intimacy. Sometimes ADHD behaviors coexist with anxiety, depression, substance abuse, or other psychiatric problems, which must be addressed as well.

When ADHD adults are involved in intimate relationships, therapy needs to include their significant others as well. A person's ADHD diagnosis may help his wife or other important person to understand him better and stop blaming him for his difficulties. But she still may need to work through her angry feelings before a better, more healthful relationship can be built.

Many adults who retain symptoms of ADHD function extremely well, despite their persisting difficulties. For some, symptoms diminish to the point that they create few problems. Others select occupations in which the ADHD-like symptoms present less of a problem. Still others develop effective coping strategies. As the parent of a child with ADHD, you hope that your child will be one of these success stories. By supporting him, focusing on his strengths rather than on his weaknesses, and taking pride in his accomplishments, you may be able to help him along that path.

CHAPTER 13

Taking Care of Yourself and Your Family

Parents of children with ADHD face multiple assaults on their own feelings of self-esteem, self-confidence, and self-worth. For starters, their often-difficult children take more time and energy than they anticipated, and despite all their efforts, nothing seems to help. Second, their children give little back; often they are unable to stop what they are doing to give Mom a hug, or to sit still long enough to enjoy a cuddle. Finally, many parents feel guilty for being too impatient, too strict, too lenient, or for a variety of other perceived parental shortcomings.

It isn't always easy to be the sister or brother of an ADHD child, either. Parents may constantly seem to be either angry or exhausted, or a little of each. Despite the fact that the sibling who has ADHD seems to be the cause of all the family turmoil, he or she is the one who gets all the attention. Meanwhile, the sibling without ADHD is expected to be good all the time, to not rock the boat, to not add to the parents' difficulties, to not antagonize the ADHD brother or sister (who is such a pain).

The management strategies discussed in this book are designed to help children with ADHD become more successful, happier, and better able to function effectively in school, at home, and elsewhere. Throughout this book, we have emphasized the importance of the family in this endeavor. In order for the ADHD child to be successful, families must work together to build a healthful environment. But families are only as strong as their individual members. Thus, parents and nonaffected siblings must also be cared for and nurtured.

By the time a family comes in to the ADHD Clinic in Philadelphia for treatment of attentional and behavioral problems, the parents often feel depleted and desperate, and sometimes depressed. One mother said she felt like a "cruise director" with her son, who was constantly into things, demanding attention, and making trouble. "We had gotten to the point where we were too tired to deal with him. We blocked him out. We felt like it was our fault," she said. Other parents report feeling weary from the constant battles they fight, not only with their children but with schools, preschools, and people who can't or won't deal with their children.

This weariness often carries over into feelings of guilt and anger. Even when parents understand the basis of their child's difficulties and the appropriate way to respond to his problems, they cannot maintain control all the time. It is hard not to wonder "Why is he doing this to me?" or "Why am I trying so hard when he doesn't appreciate my efforts?" While one inner voice may be telling you to stay calm, not get angry, and be understanding, another part of you may be outraged at the unfairness of it all.

Many parents cannot find baby-sitters willing to care for their ADHD children; they cannot go to stores, restaurants, church, or family affairs because their children's disruptive behavior embarrasses them or compels them to leave. Sometimes they lose contact with friends who don't understand the ADHD child's difficulties or the parents' struggles, and who, consequently, feel uncomfortable around the child. These friends may not want their own children around the ADHD child for fear that his behavioral problems will "rub off." They may offer "expert" advice without really understanding the depth of the problem.

The result is a feeling of isolation, which often even applies to the parents' extended family. Many grandparents and other family members do not understand ADHD or the struggles the parents face every day with their child. A grandmother may say, "I could straighten him out," or, "You just let him get away with too much." A sister may say, "I don't have that problem with my child. You must be doing something wrong." When parents try various forms of treatment, they often hear another round of advice: "He doesn't need that medicine; there's really nothing wrong with him," or, "I would *never* give Ritalin to my child."

Isolation from one's extended family can be a serious problem. Not only is it an ongoing source of frustration, unhappiness, and anxiety for you, it bodes poorly for your child. Researchers have found that parents who feel isolated are less competent in their parenting abilities than those who have good relations with extended family and friends.

REDUCING ISOLATION AND GETTING INFORMATION

Parents may be able to find help for their mounting problems in a number of ways. They need to reduce their isolation, and they need to become equipped to handle the difficulties that arise and to feel competent and powerful in handling their children. They need to become educated about the disorder itself, about the management alternatives available, and about resources available both for themselves and for their children. Parent-support groups can help by offering information as well as support. They consist of a group of parents who share their frustrations and successes, listen to each other, and offer support and encouragement. These groups exist in many areas around the country, organized through local hospitals and health-care clinics, through national organizations such as those listed in the appendix, and through less formal means.

While parent-support groups can help break down the isolation and be good sources of information, they sometimes promise more than they can deliver. When a group lacks a knowledgeable leader, misinformation can be spread as surely as good information. Further, the parents who come to these groups with horror stories need more than a place to ventilate their frustration; they need to move beyond feeling victimized. They need constructive suggestions for getting help. Beware of groups run by a leader who thinks he knows all the answers or who is very rigid in what he deems an "acceptable" approach. Remember that there are few absolute answers to many of the questions that you may have about ADHD.

FINDING HELP

Also important in managing your child effectively is to find professionals whom you trust and who are willing to work with you to find appropriate interventions for your child. Finding the right professional help can be difficult, especially if you live far away from a large metropolitan area. Ideally, you need a doctor who is knowledgeable about ADHD, who will include you in any decisions to be made regarding the care of your child, and who will be open to your questions. Keep in mind that some of your questions simply have no pat answers: "How long will my child continue to have problems?" "What is going to happen to him?" "Will he need medication for the rest of his life?" The lack of clear answers to these questions can be one of the most difficult aspects of ADHD for parents and doctors alike. Parents expect to receive firm answers from their doctors, just as doctors are accustomed to giving firm diagnoses and reasonable predictions about outcome. But with ADHD, there is room for much more clarity. Part of coming to terms with your child having ADHD is to accept the present lack of clarity.

TAKING CARE OF YOURSELF

To successfully handle your child's difficulties, you must also strengthen your own feelings of competence and self-worth.

This means taking time for yourself and for your other important relationships. A parent who is unhappy, lonely, and depressed cannot be an effective parent for long. Get therapy if you need help in working through your feelings of anger or depression. Work on your relationship with your spouse. Renegotiate your parenting responsibilities to be sure that one of you is not shouldering more of the burden than the other. If you are a single parent, try to find other sources of support. Find a skilled baby-sitter who will relieve you at times and can work effectively with all your children. Try to arrange occasional weekends away.

Extended families can be a valuable resource if they accept the path parents choose for their children. Sometimes your family members may criticize the choices you make. While you have come to accept your child's diagnosis, they may be unwilling to accept it. One mother said that her parents "don't understand ADD. They don't accept that he has a problem because he looks normal. They expect him to do things that he's not capable of doing. It took me a long time and a lot of tears to accept that I can't make him do some things, but I have accepted it."

If your extended family members are willing to learn more about ADHD, invite them to support-group meetings or therapy sessions, or offer them books or pamphlets that explain your child's difficulties. For some family members, this will not be enough. They may still see your child as normal and be unwilling to accept his limitations. You may want to limit your child's contact with those family members until they learn to adopt more realistic expectations of your child.

Similar problems can arise with friends who do not understand the disorder. Parents are sometimes reluctant to tell other parents that their child has ADHD, for fear that the label implies a whole set of irrelevant and negative connotations. You don't have to tell them! Use the label only in situations where it can benefit your child, such as in dealing with teachers and school administrators. There the label may constructively establish a framework in which they can better understand your child's difficulties.

TAKING CARE OF YOUR OTHER CHILDREN

Parents of several children may thank their lucky stars if only one child is affected by ADHD. But even unaffected children can present challenges. Sometimes an unaffected child can help parents understand that the problems of the child with ADHD are not the result of the parents' incompetence. But it is important for parents to maintain realistic expectations of the nonaffected child too. He may feel that he has to be "good" all the time because that is his designated role. Try to relieve him of that responsibility. Let him know that your love for him does not depend on his being "good" and that you do not expect him to be "good" all the time. When he acts up, understand that he may be seeking some of the attention he sees his ADHD sibling getting. Arrange the family schedule so it does not revolve solely around the ADHD child. If you are careful to give all your children regular, positive attention, problems may be avoided. If problems do arise, try looking on the bright side: One family reported that when their "good" child got caught stealing, the child with ADHD felt tremendously relieved. At last, the family's energy was not totally focused on fixing him!

Siblings' peer relationships also need consideration. They may find it difficult to invite friends over because of their brother's or sister's disruptive behavior. If this applies to your family, make special arrangements for the unaffected child. Take him and his friend out to a movie, or arrange visits when your ADHD child is not at home or is engaged in other activities.

Above all, make sure that you are not so overfocused on your child with ADHD that you ignore your other children's needs. All children have strengths as well as weaknesses. Although some of your children may not have attention deficits or behavior problems, they still need your attention.

ADVOCACY

Throughout this book, we have stressed the role that parents must play in obtaining appropriate services for their children. In other words, parents must advocate for their children. Advocating effectively means more than marching into school and demanding services. First, you must be well informed; second, you must be diplomatic; and finally, you must be vigilant.

Being informed is especially important if the professionals you are dealing with are not very knowledgeable about ADHD. You might expect your child's teacher to know better than anyone how your child should be taught, but the teacher may have had little training with or exposure to children with ADHD. As we have seen, the needs of ADHD children are not the same as the needs of learning-disabled children or children with social and emotional problems. If a teacher says that your child belongs in an LD class, make sure you understand and agree with the rationale behind that recommendation. If someone suggests that your child needs Ritalin, do not agree until you are sure that your child's needs have been adequately evaluated and that Ritalin is, in fact, the appropriate treatment. Rely on experts you trust, on your own understanding of the potential benefits of a treatment, and your knowledge of your child. No one knows that child better than you.

In all your dealings with various professionals, try to be diplomatic. Your child has a much better chance of success if everyone involved in his management is working together toward a common goal. The family-school relationship is especially important. It is almost always to your advantage for teachers to see your commitment. Most teachers are happy when parents express genuine interest in their child's performance at school. But realize the pressures that teachers are under. They teach many children each day, often with limited support. You may feel that your child's teachers have minimized his difficulties or been unwilling to accept any responsibility, but they may think they have already done more than enough. When deciding on management strategies that will involve teacher input—even if all that is required are occasional behavior reports—try to minimize the amount of extra effort you request of teachers. Be supportive of what the school and teachers are doing, and show your appreciation for any efforts they make.

When you disagree with something recommended by a professional, whether it be a school official or a doctor, be vigilant as well as diplomatic. For instance, if the school recommends an LD placement for your child but you think such a placement would be inappropriate, make your concerns known to the school officials—and don't give up. Persist in trying to find a better alternative. Make them prove to you that their decision is the correct one. Eventually you may end up agreeing with them, but you will know that the decision was made on the basis of what is best for your child, not on what is easiest for the school. If you are opposed to medication despite the recommendations of school officials or other professionals, find someone willing to help you manage your child without medication. Sometimes you may need legal assistance to ensure that your child receives appropriate care. In the appendix, we list advocacy organizations that can help you fight for your child's rights.

In sum, the process of finding appropriate interventions for your child may seem endless and sometimes discouraging. Three key factors may make success more attainable: First, maintain a positive and hopeful attitude. Second, continually monitor your child's performance throughout the various interventions. And third, be sure that the people on various fronts are working together in a coordinated manner.

Appendix

Attention-Deficit Disorders Association (ADDA)
1-800-487-2282

Established to promote public awareness of ADHD and to address the educational, psychological, and social needs of children and their families, the ADDA works to encourage more responsiveness to ADD in the academic and health-care communities. It offers support groups for children and families, and it sponsors an annual conference.

Children with Attention Deficit Disorders (CHADD)
1859 North Pine Island Road   Suite 185
Plantation, Florida 33322
(305) 587-3700

CHADD is a nonprofit, tax-exempt corporation that offers parent-support groups, in-service workshops, conferences, and meetings through its national headquarters in Florida and its chapters throughout the United States. It publishes a semiannual newsletter called *CHADDER* and a monthly newsletter called *Chadder Box.*

Coordinating Council for Handicapped Children
20 East Jackson Boulevard   Room 900
Chicago, Illinois 60604
(312) 939-3513

This advocacy group and information and referral source publishes several manuals and brochures about parent advocacy and services that are available for handicapped children. If you send a stamped, self-addressed envelope, you will receive a brochure called "Tax Guide for Parents," which outlines income tax deductions to which you may be entitled as the parent of a handicapped child.

Education Law Center
801 Arch Street   Suite 610
Philadelphia, Pennsylvania 19107
(215) 238-6970

This organization provides free legal advice regarding special education. It publishes a booklet called "Your Rights to Special Education."

Learning Disabilities Association (LDA)
(formerly the Association for Children and Adults with Learning Disabilities)
4156 Library Road
Pittsburgh, Pennsylvania 15234
(412) 341-1515

The LDA is a nonprofit national organization concerned with the education of children with learning disabilities and ADHD. It publishes *Newsbriefs* five times a year and has various state and local chapters.

National Center for Learning Disabilities (NCLD)
(formerly the Foundation for Children with Learning Disabilities)
99 Park Avenue
New York, New York 10016
(212) 687-7211

The NCLD is a fund-raising organization that sponsors research and advocacy programs for children with learning disabilities. It publishes a magazine once a year.

Orton Dyslexia Society
724 York Road
Baltimore, Maryland 21204

This educational organization sponsors conferences and provides speakers for various meetings. It publishes *Annals of Dyslexia.*

Suggested Reading List

Barkley, Russell A. *Attention Deficit Hyperactivity Disorder: A Handbook for Diagnosis and Treatment,* 2nd ed. New York: The Guilford Press, 1990.

Coleman, Wendy S. *Attention Deficit Disorders, Hyperactivity and Associated Disorders: A Book for Parents and Professionals,* 5th ed. Madison, Wisconsin: Calliope Bks, 1988.

Conners, C. Keith. *Feeding the Brain: How Foods Affect Children.* New York: Plenum, 1989.

Friedman, Ronald J., and Guy T. Doyal. *Attention Deficit Disorder and Hyperactivity,* 2nd ed. Austin, Texas: PRO-ED, 1987.

Gordon, Michael. *ADHD-Hyperactivity: A Consumer's Guide.* GSI Publications, 1990.

Kelley, Mary Lou. *School-Home Notes: Promoting Children's Classroom Success.* New York: The Guilford Press, 1990.

Lerner, Harriet Goldhor. *The Dance of Anger: A Woman's Guide to Changing the Patterns of Intimate Relationships.* New York: Harper and Row, 1985.

Patterson, Gerald R. *Living With Children: New Methods for Parents and Teachers.* Champaign, Illinois: Res Press, 1976.

Rosemond, John. *Ending the Homework Hassles: How to Help Your Child Succeed Independently in School.* Fairway, Kansas: Andrews, McMeel & Parker, 1990.

Silver, Larry B. *The Misunderstood Child: A Guide for Parents of Learning Disabled Children.* New York: McGraw-Hill, 1984.

Turecki, Stanley. *The Difficult Child: A New Step-by-Step Approach by a Noted Child Psychiatrist for Understanding and Managing Hard-to-Raise Children.* New York: Bantam, 1985.

Wender, Paul H. *The Hyperactive Child, Adolescent, and Adult: Attention Deficit Disorder Through the Lifespan.* New York: Oxford, 1987.

Notes

1   R. Maynard, "Omaha Pupils Given 'Behavior' Drug," *The Washington Post,* June 29, 1970.

2   P. Schrag and D. Divoky, *The Myth of the Hyperactive Child* (New York: Pantheon, 1975).

3   J. Biederman et al., "Retrospective Assessment of DSM-III Attention Deficit Disorder in Nonreferred Individuals," *Journal of Clinical Psychiatry* 51 (1990): 102–106.

4   A. J. Zametkin et al., "Cerebral Glucose Metabolism in Adults with Hyperactivity of Childhood Onset," *New England Journal of Medicine* 323 (1990): 1361–1366.

5   C. K. Conners, *Feeding the Brain: How Foods Affect Children* (New York: Plenum, 1989).

6   J. H. Satterfield et al., "Therapeutic Interventions to Prevent Delinquency in Hyperactive Boys," *Journal of the American Academy of Child and Adolescent Psychiatry* 26 (1987): 56–64.

7   R. A. Barkley et al., "Side Effects of Methylphenidate in Children with Attention Deficit Hyperactivity Disorder: A Systemic, Placebo-Controlled Evaluation," *Pediatrics* 86 (August 1990): 184–192.

8   R. L. Sprague and E. K. Sleator, "Methylphenidate in Hyperkinetic Children: Differences in Dose Effects on Learning and Social Behavior," *Science* 198 (1977): 1274–1276.

9   For example, Stanley Turecki, *The Difficult Child* (New York: Bantam, 1985); Gerald R. Patterson, *Living With*

NOTES · **211**

Children: New Methods for Parents (Champaign, Illinois: Res Press, 1976).

10 M. A. Atkins, W. E. Pelham, and K. J. White, "Hyperactivity and Attention Deficit Disorders," in *Psychological Aspects of Developmental and Physical Disabilities: A Casebook* (New York: Pergamon, 1990), 137–156.

11 B. J. Kaplan et al., "Dietary Replacement in Preschool-Aged Hyperactive Boys," *Pediatrics* 83 (1989): 7–17.

12 W. E. Pelham et al., "Methylphenidate and Baseball Playing in ADHD Children: Who's on First?" *Journal of Consulting and Clinical Psychology* 58 (1990): 1–4.

13 G. Weiss and L. T. Hechtman, *Hyperactive Children Grown Up* (New York: The Guilford Press, 1986).

14 R. Gittelman et al., "Hyperactive Boys Almost Grown Up: I. Psychiatric Status," *Archives of General Psychiatry* 42 (1985): 937–947.

15 S. Mannuzza et al., "Hyperactive Boys Almost Grown Up: II. Status of Subjects Without a Mental Disorder," *Archives of General Psychiatry* 45 (1988): 13–18.

Index